APPROACHES AND METHODS IN ENGLISH LANGUAGE TEACHING

(For B.Ed. Students)

Dr. (Mrs.) NAMITA ROY CHOUDHURY
M.A., M.Ed., Ph.D.

Second Revised Edition: 2013

Himalaya Publishing House

MUMBAI • NEW DELHI • NAGPUR • BENGALURU • HYDERABAD • CHENNAI • PUNE • LUCKNOW • AHMEDABAD • ERNAKULAM • BHUBANESWAR • INDORE • KOLKATA • GUWAHATI

First Edition : 2002

Second Revised Edition : 2013

Published by : Mrs. Meena Pandey for **Himalaya Publishing House Pvt. Ltd.,** "Ramdoot", Dr. Bhalerao Marg, Girgaon, **Mumbai - 400 004**. Phone: 022-23860170/23863863, Fax: 022-23877178
E-mail: himpub@vsnl.com; Website: www.himpub.com

Branch Offices :

New Delhi : "Pooja Apartments", 4-B, Murari Lal Street, Ansari Road, Darya Ganj, New Delhi - 110 002. Phone: 011-23270392, 23278631; Fax: 011-23256286

Nagpur : Kundanlal Chandak Industrial Estate, Ghat Road, Nagpur - 440 018. Phone: 0712-2738731, 3296733; Telefax: 0712-2721215

Bengaluru : No. 16/1 (Old 12/1), 1st Floor, Next to Hotel Highlands, Madhava Nagar, Race Course Road, Bengaluru - 560 001. Phone: 080-32919385; Telefax: 080-22286611

Hyderabad : No. 3-4-184, Lingampally, Besides Raghavendra Swamy Matham, Kachiguda, Hyderabad - 500 027. Phone: 040-27560041, 27550139; Mobile: 09390905282

Chennai : No. 8/2, 2nd Madley Street, Ground Floor, T. Nagar, Chennai - 600 017. Mobile: 09345345055

Pune : First Floor, "Laksha" Apartment, No. 527, Mehunpura, Shaniwarpeth (Near Prabhat Theatre), Pune - 411 030. Phone: 020-24496323/24496333; Mobile: 09370579333

Lucknow : House No 731, Shekhupura Colony, Near B.D. Convent School, Aliganj, Lucknow - 226 022. Mobile: 09307501549

Ahmedabad : 114, "SHAIL", 1st Floor, Opp. Madhu Sudan House, C.G. Road, Navrang Pura, Ahmedabad - 380 009. Phone: 079-26560126; Mobile: 09377088847

Ernakulam : 39/176 (New No: 60/251) 1st Floor, Karikkamuri Road, Ernakulam, Kochi - 682011, Phone: 0484-2378012, 2378016; Mobile: 09344199799

Bhubaneswar : 5 Station Square, Bhubaneswar - 751 001 (Odisha). Phone: 0674-2532129, Mobile: 09338746007

Indore : Kesardeep Avenue Extension, 73, Narayan Bagh, Flat No. 302, IIIrd Floor, Near Humpty Dumpty School, Indore - 452 007 (M.P.). Mobile: 09301386468

Kolkata : 108/4, Beliaghata Main Road, Near ID Hospital, Opp. SBI Bank, Kolkata - 700 010, Phone: 033-32449649, Mobile: 09883055590, 07439040301

Guwahati : House No. 15, Behind Pragjyotish College, Near Sharma Printing Press, P.O. Bharalumukh, Guwahati - 781009, (Assam). Mobile: 09883055590, 09883055536

DTP by : HPH, Editorial Office, Bhandup (Sagar Yadav)

Printed at : Geetanjali Press Pvt. Ltd., Nagpur. On behalf of HPH.

To
My Late Husband

PREFACE TO THE SECOND REVISED EDITION

Two most significant challenges essential in language teaching: teachers language proficiency and students access to immediate, authentic and copious native language samples. Teachers who teach a language in a first language environment are very often non-native speakers of that language. This demography, by and large, makes for excellent emphatic teachers who are sensitive to grammatical and social constraints between the native language and the second language.

The second major dilemma presented by English language teaching is the access to useful, appropriate and plentiful language materials in all modalities.

Policy and practice in schools is often influenced by political imperatives as well as ideas about the supposed cognition and social effects in growing up bilingual children.

Good teaching cannot be reduced to techniques. Good teaching comes from the identity and integrity of the teacher. Good teachers possess a capacity for connectedness. They are able to weave a complex web of connections among themselves – their subjects and their students so that students can learn to weave a world for themselves. The methods used by these weavers vary widely: lectures, collaborative problem solving etc. The good teachers weave the fabric that joins them with students and subjects.

If teaching cannot be reduced to techniques, it is both good news and bad news. The good news is that we no longer need to suffer the boredom that many of us feel when teaching is approached as a question of 'how to do it'. If identity and integrity are more fundamental to good teaching than techniques and if we want to grow as teachers, we must do something alien to our academic culture. Identity and integrity are subtle dimensions of the complexes demanding life-long processes of self-discovery. Identity lies in the intersection of the diverse forces that make up life and integrity lies in relating to those forces in ways that bring the wholeness rather than fragmentation.

In my second and revised edition of the 'Approaches and Methods in English Language Teaching' I have emphasized the 'Communicative Approach'. The learning of second language takes place in a variety of formal and informal situations in schools, in adult classes and at the workplace. Communicative Approach emphasizes the development of communication competence and develop the ability to become a functioning member of a cultural, occupational and professional community.

My purpose will be rewarded if my effort enriches the ability of the students and teachers of Indian schools and the readers in all contexts.

Dr. (Mrs.) Namita Roy Choudhury

PREFACE TO THE FIRST EDITION

The teaching of English language has been accorded an important position in language teaching in our schools because of its international status and its pivotal role as 'link language' to the western world.

In the schools of India the teaching of English language is a complex issue, with students coming from homes where a variety of native languages are spoken. English language teachers must recognise that under the English language teaching, there is included a variety of skills to be taught and a vast amorphous mass of material to work with, but a few obvious facts to teach. The material of English exists in the mind of the learner, who is being taught. The English teacher aims to stimulate the learner to think and to express his thoughts. He intends to stimulate the learner to feel and to become conscious of his feelings. The teacher cannot supply the thought, the teacher cannot supply the feelings. What the teacher aims to do is to put the learner into situations, real or imaginary, in which he will be compelled to think and express his thoughts.

English language teaching calls for teaching of each of the aspects of the language: Prose, Poetry, Grammar and Composition. The author has made an attempt to deal with each of these aspects from the point of view of a language teacher. It is hoped that this book will provide a useful tool to English language teachers entrusted with the task of conveying the beauty and sound of the English language to the students of Indian Schools.

The book is based on the B.Ed. (Bachelor in Education) English Method Syllabus of University of Mumbai. It is the outcome of the author's experience of decades in teaching the methodology of teaching English in the Colleges of Education at Mumbai. She has endeavoured to allow the issues, concerns and questions that typically arise in the process of teaching English to students, for whom English is a second or a third language.

English language teachers are in full agreement about the general principles and aims that should govern the teaching of English; but the work of translating them into practice must ultimately be the responsibility of the individual teachers. This book focuses the author's effort toward a student-oriented text with its clear, methodological approach. If appreciated by the readers, it will be an accomplishment for the author.

The author is grateful to her students over the past years who have helped her develop a healthy appreciation for the challenges of English language teaching in Indian schools. Their contribution to the realm of her experience has gone a long way towards writing this book.

Dr. (Mrs.) NAMITA ROY CHOUDHURY

CONTENTS

1 LANGUAGE — ITS ROLE AND FUNCTIONS

What is a language? It refers to a coding system used to organise, categories, associate, recall and retrieve information about the world. The words that make up the language system or code are shared in general by the community of language users. A language reflects the community base and the individual's experience with the real world. Individuals must learn the social base of language and conform to their communities codes, but at the same time each person's private code will be slightly different, depending on his or her learning and experience with reality.

A language is the code or symbol system that is used for communication and thought. It allows us to organize and associate information obtained as we grow older and increase our experience with the world. The language code is organized in very specific ways. Language serves as a symbolic code that manipulates, organizes and associates information and allows for efficient and appropriate recall and retrieval of information for speaking and writing.

What is the relationship of a thought and a language? Two different schools of thought exist; with some attempting a middle ground. For our one school of thought, supported by researchers such as Bruner (1964), Luria (1957) and Vygotsky (1962), language is seen to be the primary factor that composes and allows for higher forms of thought. For the other school of thought, language and thought are viewed as two separate processes. Thought is greatly facilitated by language but exists apart from it. The central issue is: as language increases in complexity, problem-solving ability goes with it. Language is perceived to be the element that allows the child to progress from sensorimotor and pre-operational thought to concrete and more abstract levels of thought (Bruner 1964). According to this view, language acts as verbal mediation. Luria (1957), perceives language as becoming more a means of self-regulation and self-control as the child matures.

Piaget was an advocate of the group, who takes the view that language and thought are independent processes. Sensorimotor activity is the foundation of thought. In other words, thought is separate from language and exists before the child begins to speak language. As the infant observes his or her world, touches, feels, tastes, hears and manipulates objects, there is a building of certain mental schemata of reality. By acting on the world, the child begins to understand and think about the world. This thought revolves around perception or imagery (mental images or pictures). After children have built these initial schemata of their world; they begin to develop language. Language is built on this action base. From this point on, language increases dramatically and is undoubtedly the best and major thought process. However, it is not the only thought process. Evidence includes a number of studies that have found that deaf children perform equivalent to normal hearing children on non-verbal measures of problem solving (Furth, 1971). Language is the means by which results of human thought and action, are passed on.

Language is a system of arbitrary, vocal symbols which permits all people in a given culture, to communicate or to interact. Every language operates within its own system, within its own recurring patterns or arrangements which are meaningful to its speaker and listener. The major functions of language have been subdivided by some linguists as follows:

(a) **Personal:** to express one's emotions, needs, thoughts, desires, attitudes, etc.

(b) **Interpersonal:** to maintain good social relations with individuals and groups - expressions of praise, sympathy, joy at another's success, etc.

(c) **Directive:** to control the behaviour of others through advice, warnings, requests, persuasion, discussion, etc.

(d) **Referential:** to talk about objects or events in the immediate setting or environment or in the culture.

(e) **Imaginative:** to use language creatively in rhyming, composing poetry, etc.

It is important to remember, that even in acquiring his native tongue, the child must be in an environment, where he hears meaningful 'noises' and where other people react to the sounds he makes. While going through the stages of language development, children must receive the primary data (meaningful speech sounds), which they will then process. Language learning means acquiring the ability to ask and answer questions; to make statements; and to produce the normal authentic forms used by native speakers. The end-result is 'free' communication. This can only be achieved, if students are helped through orderly presentation of language materials and extensive oral practice to communicate. Second language learning, however, calls for acquiring new habits or ways of using the speech organs and learning the forms and the arrangements of forms required by the system through the intensive and extensive practice of numerous examples. The sounds, forms or word sequences must be taught and practiced systematically in a progression and order which will permit the learners to associate each little segment of newly acquired language with every other segment they have already acquired.

Recent theories of second language learning indicate that conceptual processes play a major role in developing receptive and productive language skills. Research as well as theory suggests that learning strategies assists learning a second language. Studies of 'good language learners' have indicated that individuals, who have been successful in learning second language, use a variety of strategies to assist their learning. Both cognitive and metacognitive strategies have been used by second language learners to assist learning receptive and productive language skills. Among the metacognitive strategies are selective attention, monitoring, and self-evaluation. The cognitive strategies reported to be used by students include inferencing, grouping, auditory representation, note taking, and elaboration. In addition, second language learners have been found to make effective use of social/affective strategies, such as peer cooperation and questioning for clarification.

A language lives only so long as there are people who speak it, and use it as their native tongue, and its greatness lies in being given to it by these people. A language is important because the people who speak it are important - politically, economically, commercially, socially, culturally. In this context, the importance of the English language is great. Spoken by more than 340 million people in the world as a first language in the United Kingdom, the United States, and the former British Empire, it is the largest of the occidental languages. But the importance of a language is not just a matter of numbers or territory; rather it is inevitably associated in the mind of the world with the political role played by the nations using it and with their influence in international affairs; with the extent of their business enterprise and the international scope of commerce; with the conditions of life under which the great mass of these people live; and with the part played by them in art, literature and music, in science and invention, in exploration and discovery. In short, with their contribution to the all-round progress of the world. Finally, there is the practical fact that a language may be important as a *'lingua franca'* in a country or region whose diverse populations would otherwise be unable to communicate. This is specially true in the former colonies of England and France where the colonial languages have remained indispensable even after independence.

Around the world today, the most commonly taught foreign language is English. In virtually every country today, English language teaching is a major educational endeavour. Attempts at reform and change are common in English language teaching. Methodological innovations abound. The present English language reflects many centuries of development. The political and social events that have so profoundly affected the English people, have had a recognizable effect on the English language.

Since language reflects the culture of the native speakers, students should be given insight into the habits, customs, and values, which may be similar to or different from their own. It is imperative, however, that they appreciate that all people have culture and that there are no 'good' or 'bad' cultures; and that they retain pride in their own cultures as they move toward the acceptance of the language and culture of native English speakers.

The primary objective of the English teaching programmes will result inevitably from the efforts to give learners the opportunities for practice which will ensure accuracy, fluency, and appropriateness in a variety of social situations. The sequence in which the four linquistic skills taught are: listening, speaking, reading, writing. The first approach to language should be through the ear. Students should be asked to read only when they are in reasonable fluency with the reading material. The principal aim of any language lesson may be the development of one skill only, but there will be necessary overlapping with other skills. Within each of the skills, attention must be given to the sound system, the structure system, and the vocabulary. No skill is developed without continuous and intensive practice. No skill can be maintained unless it is used frequently. The planning for continuous and intensive practice in which the study material is constantly reintroduced and consolidated with known material, constitute one of the major responsibilities of the teacher of English as a second language.

HPH

2 LISTENING

The goal of listening is comprehension. So it is essential that listening activities attract and hold the attention of students so that they are motivated to listen carefully. Listening practice is specially important in classrooms where English is taught as a second or third language.These students often learn to read and write English, but they frequently have great difficulty comprehending English spoken to them.

The first step in teaching the listening skill is to accustom students to the 'noise' of the language. This early stage is best accomplished by what is referred to as 'selective listening.' The students must concentrate on certain features of the language at a time, and in order to do this systematically and efficiently, selective listening should be employed. This 'selective listening' can be as specific as teaching the discrimination of sounds, both in words and sentences:

Washing She is washing the car.

Watching She is watching the car.

Listening is, in many ways, more exacting than reading. Listening, like reading, is a receptive skill. The listener, like the reader, can translate experience into thought on several levels. The reader can stop, look up a word, reflect; he can slow down when the information is dense or the exposition difficult; he can even re-read complex passages. The listener, of course, has no such advantages. However, listening, like reading, is of various types, each of which must be mastered through practice. Careful listening, like careful reading, involves attending to what is being communicated. But listening demands on the grammatical as well as the lexical skills of the listener. Because English is not his native language, the language-learner is less able to predict the pattern of a sentence through its initial grammatical signals. Listening to a foreign language may be analysed as involving two kinds of activities; both of which must be taught. The first: the recognition level, which involves the identification of words and phrases in their structural relationships, of time sequences, and of phrases which are redundant interpolations, adding nothing to the development of the line of thought. The second: the level of selection, where the listener is drawing out from the communication of those elements, which seem to him to contain the gist of the message. This process requires him to concentrate his attention on certain sound groupings while others are aurally perceived without being retained. For the student to be able to listen with ease to the foreign language in normal situations, he need thorough training at the recognition level and much practice in selecting specific details from the stream of sound. Training at the recognition level must begin from the first lesson. This does not mean the presentation of unguarded and ill-designed aural material for the language learner. In the considerably few hours at the disposal of the teacher in the classroom, methods must be adopted which will lead more directly to the objective, i.e., developing the greatest degree of listening skill possible in the time available.

For a method to be economical as well as efficient, it must take into account all the skill elements which should be developed. In a listening situation, the student must be familiar with the components of a stream of speech that he can react quickly to some of them and pass rapidly over others which are redundant or irrelevant to his immediate purpose. He must be able to recognise without effort, sound patterns, grammatical sequences and tenses, function words, expletives or hesitation expressions, as well as social or dialectical variations. As these aspects of speech become familiar to the student, his expectation of their use in certain contexts rises and their information content is, as a consequence, lessened. As the human organism is able to absorb only a certain amount of information at one time, this familiarity, by decreasing the information content, increases the number of items with which the student can cope in one utterance. Systematically prepared listening comprehension materials will provide training, in a steady progression, for the listening skill of the language-learner. If suitable materials are not available, the language teacher will choose, adopt and re-fashion those which are obtainable or prepare his own, with the basic requirements in mind.

The purpose of extensive listening practice is to give the learner plenty of opportunities to develop and exercise his listening skills in as natural way as possible. Extensive listening need not be tested in detail. The learner will be following the meaning of the listening passage, because he is interested in the information contained in it, or simply because he is enjoying it. What would extensive listening materials sound like? Obviously, this depends on the level of learner that they are intended for, but it is important that they should be varied. Recordings of stories and other texts, taken from books or magazines, can often be used. For the more advanced learners, it is rather important to get away from language that has been specially controlled for teaching purposes. Recordings from radio and television are good sources of spontaneous conversation. Variety in listening materials will make the listening interesting to language learners. Should the language content of the listening passages be controlled? The answer depends on how advanced in their study of the language the pupils are. It is important that extensive listening materials should not slavishly follow the set syllabus of a teaching course, which would defeat the purpose of the exercise. There should be not only familiar words and phrases in new contexts, but also new words and phrases which the pupil has to try to make sense of.

How should extensive listening practice be prepared for? Ideally, a period of extensive listening, particularly in lower level classes, would be introduced by familiarising the pupils with the general context of the listening passage by looking at a photograph or a picture, asking one or two questions about it and making sure that they know the meaning of some of the key items which can be seen in the picture or define verbally. The purpose of this introductory work, which will not take long nor go into great details, is to put the pupils in the right frame of mind for the listening practice and thus make it much easier for them to make sense of the language that they are going to hear. The term 'key items' is not synonymous with 'useful English words.' They are items which, in a particular passage, play a specially significant role in the structure of the passage, so that a failure to understand them is very likely to lead to a failure to understand a large section of the passage, if not all of it. These items must be known before the pupils do the listening practice, or they must be made very clear from the context, with the use of sound effects in the recording or the histrionic abilities of the speakers. To listen effectively is not just a question of recognition and passive absorption. The listener should be mentally checking, supporting, challenging and extrapolating the items of information, contained in the discourse. Aural analysis rarely receives systematic or thorough training in classroom teaching. This training is urgently required for effective listening skill.

3 SPEAKING

The primeval form of language is 'speech,' a fact taken as first principle by the advocates of the Direct Method, who directed language-teaching research in the first half of the twentieth century. Speaking is a more complex skill than listening. In addition to knowing the sound, structure and vocabulary, the speakers must (a) think of the ideas they wish to express, (b) change the tongue, lip and jaw positions in order to articulate the appropriate sounds, (c) consciously aware of the appropriate functional expression as well of the grammatical, lexical, and cultural features needed to express the idea, (d) be sensitive to any change or style necessitated by the persons to whom they are speaking and the situation in which the conversation is taking place, (e) change the direction of their thoughts on the basis of the other person's responses. All of these are interrelated acts, which must take place instantaneously and simultaneously. Spontaneous and creative use of language may develop only after years of learning, depending upon the age, motivation, and aptitude of the learner and on the quality of instruction.

Logically there are three steps in teaching speech: inculcating the phonological system; teaching pupils how to manipulate structures; and conditioning pupils to use their skills with ease. Language teaching begins with the spoken language. Material is taught orally before it is presented in written form. The oral approach was the accepted approach to English language teaching by the 1950s. One of the most active proponents of the Oral Approach in the sixties was George Pittman. Pittman and his colleagues were responsible for developing an influential set of teaching materials based on the situational approach, which were widely used in Australia, New Guinea and the Pacific territories.

We use speech in most human activities. We use speech to convey information from one person to another, carry on conversations, expound on favourite topics, etc. Hymes (1972), has proposed a useful distinction between speech situations, speech events and speech acts. Within a community one finds many situations associated with speech. The term 'speech event' can be restricted to activities that are directly governed by rules or norms for the use of speech: lectures, introductions, religious discourses and the like. Speech acts, in a narrow sense, are the minimal terms of the set: speech situation/event/act. When we speak we perform acts, such as giving reports, making statements, asking questions, making promises, approving and apologising. It is unquestionably assumed that a 'living' language is basically speech. This assumption derives from appreciation of the social and dynamic aspects of language. It is speech, which serves as the natural means of communication between members of a community, both for the expression of thought and as a form of social behaviour.

Main features of speech:

(a) Speech, as conversation, implies a speaker-listener situation with alternating roles.

(b) Speech, as conversation, requires the spontaneous application of language habits.

(c) The signaling devices available to the speaker, apart from word and sentence structure, are gesture, word-stress and intonation.

4 THE SOUND OF ENGLISH: INTONATION

Spoken English has led us to realise the importance of stress, pitch, and pause in signaling meanings in English. When the language-learner understands the patterns of intonation in spoken English and the relationship of the sound-signal system of punctuation, he can gain a firmer grasp of the language. The teacher can help him understand the importance of intonation, pitch, and stress in the spoken language by asking them to read the printed symbols in varying ways. He can see how many different meanings can be implied by the voice with the same symbols. Although the complexities of intonation in English speech are too many for the language-learner to master completely, there are some important ways in which the study of sound patterns can help him in writing. The patterns of intonation serve as an invaluable guide in clarifying the ambiguities of meaning; they often offer clues to punctuation, and they serve to help the learner sense the structure of English language sentences. The three parts of the intonation system of English are stress, pitch and juncture. Stress indicates the degree of loudness or softness of the syllables being uttered. The variation in tones of voice from low to high in English speech is called pitch. The pauses in the stream of speech sounds make up the system of juncture in English intonation.

Recognition of intonation patterns can help the learner in punctuation. The learner who can master the high-low intonation patterns of the declarative sentence, has grasped a basic concept about sentence structure and punctuation. Since intonation indicates important syntactic relationships in English, the learner who masters the essentials of the system, understands more clearly the structures he reads and writes. Intonation provides some of the most helpful clues to the recognition of sentence fragments. As he trains his ear to observe the way his voice works in the intonation of the sentence patterns he utters, he understands how to read by structural patterns rather than single words, and how to write and punctuate by the syntactical groupings of words in sentences.

Mastering Punctuation

Punctuation attempts to substitute written symbols for the pauses, stresses and pitch of the spoken language. The two reasons for learning to punctuate are: (a) to convey written thoughts with accuracy, and (b) to appear literate and educated to the audience for which one writes. The simple rules to help the learner in this regard are: (1) Do not overpunctuate. When in doubt, leave the punctuation mark out. (2) Do observe current usage in punctuation.

HPH

5 PLACE OF THE ENGLISH LANGUAGE IN THE SCHOOL CURRICULUM

Language is considered to be a means of communication through a system of symbols. In society, language is an essential requirement. It joins man to man by way of greetings, conversation, inquiries, discussion and opposition. Language has, thus, a broader scope - it is a means of social control. Ideas emerge and materialize through language.

In the classroom and in school, language has a two-fold role to play. It serves as a vehicle of thought and communication for acquiring knowledge. In addition, language is shielded for its own sake. The imbibing of a nation's culture, traditions and customs is achieved through the study of language.

Language as a Means of Intellectual, Emotional and Social Development

Human language has kept pace with the growth of civilization. In the same way, language keeps pace with the growth of individual man. Speech is essentially a human faculty. The process of the early development of language is purely imitative and wholly conscious under normal circumstances. The intellectual growth is shaped by the language habits formed by the child through interrelation with society. The growth of the child's intellect is made possible through language - a medium of knowledge, tradition and culture. The language rich in literature and tradition, is of tremendous value to the intellectual and emotional development of an individual.

Language is not only a means whereby we make statements and express our thoughts and ideas about things. We actually think by means of language. Our ability to think, as well as our ability to express our thoughts, is limited by our ability to use language. Our understanding the thoughts of other people is limited by our own ability to use language ourselves. In addition, language is one of the means whereby we express our feelings.

Present Position of Teaching Languages in School Curriculum

The Constitution of India as adopted in 1950, had envisaged Hindi as the only language of the Union of India while English was to continue for fifteen years. This was opposed by the states in the South. As a result, English was adopted as the Associate official language by an Act of Parliament in 1963. The position given to English in the school curriculum was laid down by the Kothari Commission (1964-1966). The school syllabi in most Indian states, have been framed, based on the recommendations of the Kothari Commission. The objectives of teaching English underwent a change under the present conditions. The teaching of English is made more practical and language-oriented in order to achieve the limited objectives; as pointed out by an Official Language Commission English has to be taught hereafter principally as 'language of comprehension rather than as literary language.'

The Kothari Commission has assigned the most important position of the first language to the mother-tongue from pedagogical and psychological point of view. Hindi has been assigned the position of a compulsory second language in view of the fact that it is the national language of India. English has been given the position of third language in the school curriculum.

Role of English Language in the School

The three language formula envisages compulsory study of English either as a second or third language for a period of six years. English as the third language (L3) may be introduced either in Class V or Class VIII. The medium of instruction at the University Level continues to be English until the regional Indian language had been enriched to replace it for higher scientific and technical education.

The three-language formula seems to be in keeping with the latest trends in language learning all over the world. Modern researches conducted by the UNESCO in many developing countries have shown that education has to be three dimensional. It has to teach:

(a) A mother-tongue in order to create an individual's personals identity,

(b) A national language for the purpose of national unity,

(c) A foreign language as a basis for international cooperation and free exchange of ideas.

The Aims and Objectives of Teaching English at the School Level

We must recognize that under the heading 'English,' there is included a variety of skills to be taught and vast mass of material to work with, but very few obvious facts to teach. In answer to the question what it is that we 'teach' under the subject 'English,' we can only answer in a general way that we teach English language in all its forms. We teach the language itself and discuss how it is constructed. We teach how the language can be spoken in various ways, how it can be reproduced for other person's thoughts and feelings. We teach how the language can be written down and how various ways of writing can have various effects on the minds of those who read. We teach our pupils how to read so that they can understand what is written and we train them to listen so that they can understand what the speaker wishes to convey. We train them to be sensitive to the beauties of spoken and written language.

Language is not only a means whereby we make statements and express our thoughts and ideas about things. More than this, we actually think by means of language. Our ability to think as well as our ability to express our thoughts, is limited by our own ability to use language ourselves. In addition, language is one of the means, whereby we express our feelings.

The aim of the teacher of English will be two-fold: (a) to increase the ability of his pupils over language which deals with ideas and to increase their ability over language which expresses feelings. A teacher of English should be an expert in both of these uses of language. From his extensive use of language every pupil will bring to the English lesson a set of language habits formed to express themselves more clearly and to correct those habits which impede or which are not socially acceptable. Teaching of English must always be adjusted to the level of emotional and intellectual development of the pupils. English language offers enormous quantities of material of all stages and of all levels of thought and feelings and therefore calls for the ability to select the material which is suitable to a group of children at a particular time and at their particular level of development. The aim of the teacher is to put the learner into situations, real or imaginary, in which he will be compelled to think or feel in a particular way. The teaching of an English teacher is consequently based on a direct contact with the feelings and thoughts of his pupils. He acts as simulator, as a guide, and as a refining agent for the learner's thoughts and ideas, feelings and imagination.

The ultimate aims are clear: good listening, good speaking, good reading and good writing. These should continue all through the school level and not one of them should be neglected, though there are stages when one or other may require special emphasis.

Objectives of Teaching English

Language learning consists of certain skills. There are four fundamental skills which are basic to a language. The four skills are Understanding, speaking, reading and writing. They are the four fundamental objectives of teaching English.

The first of these skills is (a) **Understanding:** What is spoken. Understanding requires listening and forms a part of it. As compared to the skill of speaking, understanding is rather passive but is a wider skill. The achievement of this skill would result in bringing about certain changes in the behaviour of the pupils, who would be able to follow English sounds in speech, would be able to understand new words and sentence patterns in speech and writing. (b) **Speaking:** Speech is essential because language is a spoken thing. The changes in the speech behaviour with proper accent and intonation, answering question using new words and structures, expressing thoughts orally in correct language. (c) **Reading:** The ability of recognizing words. The behaviour changes of the pupils would result in reading with expression, in silent reading, extracting quickly the meaning underneath. (d) **Writing:** Learning a language usually has a practical aim to enable student to communicate in that language. Writing calls for presenting the information in written form in legible handwriting with correct punctuation marks.

Within these main skills there are a large number of secondary skills, which often overlap and reinforce one another.

Principles of Language Learning

Ben Johnson wrote that speech was the 'instrument of society.' Only careful and systematic training in the correct use of speech will enable our pupils to play their role in a democratic society. Only careful and systematic training in the actual sounds and manners of speech (speech training) will enable them to present their ideas clearly to hold the attention and interest of their listeners.

I. Imitation: Language is learnt through imitation. It is specially true in the case of younger children.

II. Practice and Drill: Language-learning is a habit formation process. Habits are formed through repetition, which calls for continuous practice and drill work. All aspects of language learning, i.e., listening, speaking, reading, and writing can be acquired after great deal of practice.

III. Oral Approach: Language is related to ears and tongue. In the teaching of language, oral work should be given topmost priority. A language should be learnt by speaking it. Living language should be thought as living speech, i.e., they should be taught orally.

IV. Selection and Gradation: In the teaching of a language, selection and gradation of language items are very important. The selection of language items should be based on the following principles:

(a) Frequency of language item and its occurrence.

(b) Range of applicability, i.e., applicability in how many contexts.

(c) Coverage a word conveying a number of meaning, e.g.,the word 'meal' stands for breakfast, dinner, etc.

(d) Availability - language items which can be conveniently taught, e.g., classroom subjects, like chair, table, desk, chalk, etc.

(e) Teachability -language items which are easy from teaching point of views.

(f) Learnability - language items, easy for the learners to learn should be taken up first.

Gradation means putting language items in order of presentation. Gradation involves grouping and sequence.

(a) Grouping

(i) According to sound, e.g., pat, bat, cat; which is called phonetic grouping. (ii) According to the words used in the same situation, e.g., words connected with post office - postmaster, postman, letter; which is called lexical grouping. (iii) Patterns of sentences, which are similar, e.g., this is, that is, my book, your book; called grammatical grouping. (iv) Semantic grouping includes the words which convey similar meanings, e.g., shelter, hut, house, tent etc. (v) Structure grouping puts the selected items to fit with each other - sounds into words, words into phrases, phrases into sentences and sentences into context.

(b) Sequence

(i) Lexical sequence: words which follow, e.g., sit, stand, come, go. (ii) Grammatical sequence: these words are put in order and are taught at different occasions, e.g., the word 'there.'

(a) The pen is there. (place)

(b) There are many pens. (introduction)

V. Motivation or Interest: Motivation or interest is of great importance in the teaching-learning process. Language is learnt quickly if interest is created in it. So the teacher should make use of effective teaching aids for this purpose.

VI. Natural Way of Teaching-Learning: Natural process of learning the language should be followed. Listening and speaking should precede reading and writing. Teachers should lay more emphasis in the beginning on listening and speaking.

VII. Language should be learnt in context and situation: The purpose of language-learning is to make use of it in day to day life-situations.

VIII. Adoption of Multiple Line of Approach: While teaching a foreign language, the multiple line of approach should be followed as it helps the learner. For example, while teaching composition writing, there should be oral work first, followed by writing some sentences on the topic in their notebooks. Spelling practice should be given from the same topic. Thus, the approach to language-learning should be many-sided.

IX. Balanced Approach: While teaching language, listening, speaking, reading and writing should be equally emphasized as far as possible.

X. Maxims of Teaching the Language: Language-learning is essentially a matter of forming correct habits of thinking and articulation. In language teaching, teacher should follow the following maxims:

(i) **Proceed from known to unknown:** The learning of different structures of the language should be based on structures previously learnt.

(ii) **Proceed from easy to difficult:** Easy and familiar words should be taught first, followed by more difficult ones.

(iii) **Proceed from simple to complex:** It is particularly useful for grading of structure and vocabulary. It is also useful for selecting material for teaching, keeping in view the age and standard of the pupils.

(iv) **Proceed from concrete to abstract:** Children learn more effectively when they can see and handle objects. Audio-visual aid (pictures, models, tape-recorders, slides, movies, etc.) should play a significant role in the teaching-learning process.

(v) **Proceed from particular to general:** The particular is always more definite than the general, which is indefinite. The particular facts should be grouped in such a manner that the children should be able to arrive at generalizations on their own. The maxim is followed in the teaching of grammar on inductive lines.

(vi) **Proceed from analysis to synthesis:** Analysis is particularly useful in the teaching of spellings where long words are broken up into its various components. It is also useful in the teaching of pronunciation and in teaching grammar. Substitution tables provide good opportunities for analyzing structures and for drill-work in using them in actual practice.

(vii) **Proceed from psychological to logical:** Teaching must always be related to the needs, interests and abilities of the learner. Hence the psychological readiness of the learner must be kept in mind before any formal teaching can take place. The psychological preparation must lead to logical approach. For the younger children, the greatest appeal can be made through story telling, nursery rhymes and jingles. Stress should be laid on deriving pleasure from language-learning.

(viii) **Proceed from empirical to rational:** Empirical knowledge is that which is based on observation. Language-learning is effective when we begin with what we can see and feel than with abstract ideas. (Structures that can be demonstrated in action, e.g., I am opening a book).

(ix) **Proceed from whole to part:** It is better to deal with a poem as a whole first before breaking it up into parts in order to enjoy the full beauty of the poem. This principle is in keeping with Gestalt theory of learning which emhasizes the importance of observing situation as a whole.

(x) **Proceed from actual to representatives:** Real objects appeal to the children. A teacher of English should make full use of the daily experiences of children for their discussion of topics in composition writing. The teaching of English structures should be based on the actual experiences of the pupils.

The aims of teaching English include (A) Reception and (B) Expression. A language is taught to enable the learners to receive it so that they are enabled to express through it properly.

(A) Reception

(i) Listening: In language-learning situation, the first important thing is listening. The teacher should give maximum listening practice to the students. He may use radio, tape-recorder, record-player, etc. for this purpose. Practice in listening is the first and foremost principle in language learning.

(B) Expression

(i) Speaking: Speaking ability in a language certainly depends upon the listening practice.

(ii) Reading: Reading is a mode of expression. It should be given due importance in the teaching of English.

(iii) Writing: An important means of expression. Learning of a language remains incomplete without the writing aspect.

The aims of teaching English may be categorised into functional aims and cultural aims.

Functional Aims

(1) To develop skills in listening to English as speech of a standard suitable to the physical, mental and emotional development of the learners.

(2) To develop skills in oral expression as a basis for learning to read and write.

(3) To develop skills in reading English as a natural step towards developing skills in writing.

(4) To develop skills in writing English so that these skills may prove the practical value in situations in which writing is needed.

Cultural Aims

(5) To develop an understanding of, appreciation for, and a desirable attitude towards the manners, customs and of cultural background of English-speaking people as an integral part of the linguistic aims, so that:

(a) In developing skills in listening, oral expression, reading and writing, the experience may be in harmony with the modes of life, manners and customs of English-speaking people, whose language comprises an integral part of their culture.

(b) The development of such an understanding, appreciation and attitude may form a foundation for those desiring to take more advanced work in language-learning beyond the higher secondary school level.

(c) The development of such an understanding, appreciation and attitude, along with the linguistic skill acquired, may contribute towards the student's individual, social and vocational competence.

(d) To develop a knowledge of English language with special attention to the sound system and the structural patterns, so that this knowledge may contribute to mastery in listening, oral expression, reading and writing and to develop an understanding of, appreciation for, and a desirable attitude towards the manners, customs and general cultural background of English speaking people, as an integral part of the linguistic aim.

Structural linguistics has long been the chief framework underlying the development of language curricula. The assumptions underlying each structuralist approaches to language syllabus design can be summarized as follows:

- The basic units of a language curriculum are vocabulary and grammar.
- Learners' needs are identified exclusively in terms of language needs.
- The classroom and the textbook provide the primary input to the language learning process and the goal of the syllabus designer is to simplify and rationalize this input through selection and gradation.
- These assumptions had influenced the design of language syllabus and pedagogy until the 1970s, when functional linguistics became the strongest rival of traditional structural linguistics.

Methods and Approaches of Teaching English to whom English is a Non-cognate

I.C. Richards (2001), summarized the different teaching methods which characterized different periods in the past century.

1. Grammar – Translation Method (1800-1900)
2. Direct Method (1890-1930)

3. Structural Method (1930-1960)
4. Reading Method (1920-1950)
5. Audio-lingual Method (1950-1970)
6. Situational Method (1950-1970)
7. Communicative Approach (1970-present)
   (a) Approaches before the 1970s are largely structure-drill based. Behaviourist theories of language learning had emphasized the function of accurate language behaviour through habit formation based on practice and drills of structures.
   (b) The structure of a foreign language is best learnt when compared and contrasted with that of the mother tongue.

A. Grammar-Translation Method

Translation is a powerful means in the teaching of a foreign language with precaution that ought to be taken not to do it in excess. The advantages are: (i) vocabulary can be acquired economically and effectively, (ii) it helps in giving a speedy comprehension. The disadvantage of this method lies in its inability to understand English as speech in its spoken form. It fails as general method of teaching pupils to express in English language.

B. Natural Method

It represented the first reaction against the grammar-translation method, but its weakness lies in the fact that it was based on the manner in which a child learns his mother tongue without realizing that a child learning a foreign language is in a different situation. A child embarking on a study of a foreign language has reached a stage of physical, mental, emotional growth and development and has acquired a language consciousness and language habits that have definite psychological influence on the acquisition of a foreign language. Because psychology was very much in its infancy at the time, the natural method became the vogue.

C. Psychological Method

A step ahead of the Natural Method as it bases its techniques on the association of ideas and the habit of mental visualization. The name chiefly connected with this method is that of Francois Gouin. The masterpiece,

'English through Actions,' which is the world of Dr. Palmer and his daughter, is based on this method. Because the lessons consist of a series of actions, it is also known as the Series method.

No method is effective if it is not used consistently. Some of the text books for beginners in English, introduce a series only once. This shows a complete lack of understanding of the whole purpose of this method.

D. Reform or Phonetic Method

Those who claim to favour a scientific approach declare that the first thing to master the language is its sound system. A careful study of the language will convince that phonetics has a very important place in language learning process.

E. Direct Method

It came as a reaction to the Translation Method. Its basic principles lies in the fact that learners should think directly in the foreign language. **Aim of Direct Method:** Establishing a direct bond between thought and expression. The language-learner should experience the new language in the same way in which he experiences his mother tongue.

Principles of Direct Method

I. Oral Training: Learning is provided with sufficient practice in listening to the language and speaking it. It also lays emphasis on the knowledge of phonetics to acquire an intelligible pronunciation. Oral training helps in the direct association of the words of the foreign language with the object and ideas for which they stand.

II. Inhibition of the Mother Tongue: Securing a direct bond between experience and expression is to inhibit the mother tongue. Pupils are taught new words by actually showing them the objects for which they stand. This helps the pupils to think in English, to respond directly in the foreign language.

III. Sentence as the Unit of Speech: Teaching through Direct Method starts with the teaching of sentences and not individual words.

IV. Inductive Teaching of Grammar: In Direct Method, grammar is taught as a means to an end. Pupil learns the language first and then the grammatical forms of the language. Direct Method does not prescribe any special method for the teaching of formal grammar and the method usually followed is the Inductive Method.

V. Teaching of New Vocabulary After Careful Selection and Gradation: Controlled vocabulary is taught in different stages of learning. Direct Method gives the pupil facility in understanding English. It helps to acquire fluency in speech. It facilitates reading and writing fairly, quickly and correctly.

Advanced linguists do not question the virtues of the Direct Method. In fact, they declare that as a method, it is the best. However, it is also known that if badly handled, the result can be very uneven. The teacher should have a complete knowledge of the structural contexts. Lessons are organized around language structures. No translation is used, although occasional directions or explanations may be given in the pupil's mother tongue.

F. Dr. West's New Method

Dr. Michael West, a former Director of Education of pre-independence Bengal, made a careful study of the teaching of English in India and devised his own method which came as a reaction against the Direct Method and its limitations. Dr. West, in his new method, attached a great deal of importance to reading. According to Dr. West, Indian pupils need the ability to read English first, then to write it and lastly to speak it and understand it when spoken. So this method gives emphasis on pupils'reading. Reading involves a kind of inner speech. So reading helps speaking. According to Dr. West 'Reading language is by far the shortest road of learning to speak and write it.' Reading is of various types. According to Dr. West, teacher of English should mainly be concerned with the teaching of silent reading as it develops comprehension and creates desire for further reading. This method does attach importance to oral work but the oral work is viewed as a preparatory step for developing the art of silent reading. Dr. West classified the words into categories: (a) structural words, i.e., the words which make up the structure of the language, (b) context words, i.e., the context of the words that we talk about. Most of the context words are nouns. Dr. West recommended a minimum speaking vocabulary of 1158 words, which are adequate for ordinary conversation. Dr. West provided series of Readers which contained interesting reading material with controlled vocabulary. For testing the efficiency of the reading, each Reader contained test in comprehension.

With its overemphasis on developing reading skill, writing skill is neglected. Oral work is not emphasized. It is looked upon as a preparation for silent reading.

G. The Structural Approach

The Structural Approach is the outcome of the extensive researches made in the field of teaching of English as foreign language. The basic principles and techniques of the Structural Approach and Direct Method are more or less the same. The method used is the Direct Method, which is based on a properly laid down graded structural syllabus. Structures may be defined as the tools of language. Just as a Carpenter works on his tools, in much the same way, the teaching and learning processes of a language are worked upon by its structures. A structure is a sentence-pattern or a linguistic frame. It is the way of arranging words in a sentence. The sentence is the smallest unit of language.

Each language has its own pattern of structures. One of the great advance in the field of linguistic science is the discovery of how the words are put together. A structural syllabus concentrates on the handling of structural words - words such as prepositions, pronouns, auxiliary verbs, conjunctions and some adverbs form the skeleton of the language; while flesh and blood is provided by the content words. Structural words are the most important words in a language but they are also the most difficult to learn for correct usage.

Experimental investigations and research have brought to light that there are 275 language-patterns which constitute the core of essential English. These language-patterns are called structures. These structures are carefully graded so that the cumulative approach will give the young learner a working command of spoken and written English at the end of the course.

In grading structures, attention is paid to both meaning and form. A graded structural syllabus sets out the most important structures in an order, considered suitable for teaching and learning.

Structural Approach is based on the following principles:

(a) Speech is the most essential means of gaining mastery over the language. Therefore, oral work should become the corner-stone of all teaching-learning process.

(b) In the process of language learning, it is the pupils' activity which is more important than the teacher's activity. Therefore, pupils should be made to act, both mentally and physically.

Besides these principles, the Structural Approach follows the principles of language teaching, enumerated by Mr. H.E. Palmer. They are as follows:

(a) Principle of Selection: Structures and content words are carefully selected. The selection is determined by the objectives of the approach, i.e., the practical command of the language, age, mental capacities and average experiences of the pupils. As stated earlier, 275 structures are selected.

(b) Principle of Gradation: The structures selected for teaching and learning of English should be well graded. The maxims, 'easy to difficult' and 'concrete to abstract' are followed for teaching graded structures.

(c) Principle of Teachability: As far as possible structures should be demonstrated in life-like situations. Such a demonstration make a structure teachable. (Situational Teaching).

(d) Principle of Opportunities for Use: The pupils should have many opportunities for using the structures which would help habit-formation in pupils because of repetition and drill work.

(e) Principle of Proportion: It is applied to the number of structures and content words to be taught in each standard, as well as the standard of attainment in each of the four linguistic skills.

Characteristic Features of the Structural Approach:

(a) Structural Approach is a psychologically sound approach, which seeks to teach four language skills, *viz.*, listening and understanding, speaking, reading and writing, in graded order.

(b) Structural approach emphasizes 'ear before eyes' and 'speech before reading and writing.' Pupils are made to listen to English and repeat the new structure several times. Then they are encouraged to make sentences of their own. It is for this reason, this approach is called an oral-aural approach.

(c) This approach makes sentences a unit of teaching. Pupils learn sentences couched in the form of structures. Therefore, they develop the ability to communicate in complete sentences.

(d) Through this approach, pupils are made to attain mastery over an essential vocabulary of 3000 content words.

(e) This approach recommends language before grammar, i.e., the mastery of the languages over the mastery of theoretical grammar. Thus, it recommends 'functional grammar'.

This approach is highly learner-centered approach. It takes the psychology of the learner into account and emphasizes the learners' activities in the teaching-learning process.

H. Teaching-learning through Structural Approach

(i) Pupils learn to recognize and understand the spoken English word. Teacher creates a meaningful situation to use the structure and repeat it several times.

(ii) Pupils learn to pronounce English words or structure by imitation. Teacher carries out individual and chorus drilling to develop speaking ability of the pupils.

(iii) Pupils learn to recognize and pronounce the written English structure and content words. After sufficient oral drilling, teacher writes the complete structure on B.B., which develops oral reading of the pupils.

(iv) Pupils learn to write the structure in their notebooks. Their writing skill is developed.

Structural Approach is most scientific, psychological and sound educational approach as it follows the principles of language-learning. It makes pupils keen and active in the learning. It is difficult to implement in Indian schools because of overcrowded classes, fixed syllabus and traditional examination system. Since this approach requires plenty of audio-visual aids in classroom teaching, it is rather expensive for Indian schools. Finally, it should be noted that the Structural Approach, to be effective enough, requires skilful and imaginative language teachers.

I. Oral Approach

Teaching English at the initial stages should be based on the oral approach. Mr. C.R. Fries regards this approach as the most economical and effective way of teaching the beginners.

Sounds, words and structures are the basic language material. If they are not mastered at the oral-aural level (speaking-listening), the language will not be learnt properly and students will develop the tendency to translate every word. There is greater need to listen to the proper pronunciation of the word and then to use the word in the spoken form.

Oral Approach emphasizes teaching every new word or structure, first by presenting it orally and then through reading and writing. Learners should learn every new item first by listening, and then by speaking; reading and writing should come thereafter.

Oral Approach covers the following aspects:

A. Adequate Ear-training

- Ample opportunities to listen to the language-sounds.

B. Imitation

- Students are encouraged to imitate the teacher's language sounds.

C. Oral Practice

- Provisions of enough oral practice by using the teaching item in various suitable situations.

Foreign language teachers all over the world agree that the oral method of teaching is the best method for both children and adults alike. Language is obviously speech before it is anything else.

J. Situational Approach

A structure or a word becomes meaningful for the learners when it is used in an appropriate situation. Language teacher should use a particular situation in order to (a) practice the structure and to relate it to its meaning, (b) to build up a vocabulary of content words.

In the early stage of language-learning everyday classroom situation should be used to familiarize the words, such as boy, girl, teacher, pupil, desk, pen, pencil, door, window, etc. Teacher must take greatest care to make the situation appropriate to a particular structure. Situations can be built up in the following ways: (i) by gestures and actions, (ii) by the use of pictures, (iii) by drawing on the blackboard.

K. The Substitution Table

In recent years a powerful device has been placed in the hands of the teacher of English as an international language. It goes to the credit of Mr. H.E. Palmer who brought the Substitution Table idea to the attention of language teachers of the world. He defines substitution 'a process by which any model sentence may be multiplied indefinitely by substituting for any of its words or word-groups of the same grammatical family and within certain semantic limits.' Mr. Palmer himself prepared 100 Substitution Tables, which can be classified in categories according to their grammatical contents.

The underlying principle of the Substitution Table Method implies that the study of a word apart from its sentence structures does not help the pupils in forming correct linguistic habits.

There are three types of Substitution Tables: (i) Simple, (ii) Compound and (iii) Grammatical Substitution Tables.

When a particular Structural item has been taught, pupils can be asked to construct sentences from the suitable substitution tables as follows:

Example:

A dog		bigger		a cat
A man	is	taller	than	a child
A week		longer		a day

A simple Substitution Table on the model S-V (She died) first offers substitution for the Subject:

Example:

S	V
She	died

The man

One of the soldiers

None of them

The ant

then offer substitutes for the Verb:

S	V
She	died. went away. disappeared. fell into the river. came near me.

When these two variations are put into the Table, 25 sentences are possible by combining any S with any V:

S	V
She The man One of the soldiers None of them The ant	died. went away. disappeared. fell into the river. came near me.

Examples:

The man came near me.

One of the soldiers fell into the river.

The ant died.

None of them went away.

Such Tables provide the simplest, quickest and most efficient method of work of five aspects of the teaching of English at any level of instruction. They can be used for:

(i) teaching a new construction;

(ii) teaching a new use of, or an elaboration of, construction already known;

(iii) Teaching a correct usage where an incorrect form tends to become a 'common error';

(iv) teaching the correct employment of the English tenses (always a troublesome subject);

(v) The permanent removal of 'common errors' as these reveal themselves in the course of routine class work.

Teaching through substitution tables ensures the formation of correct speech-habits and pupils easily acquire command over phrases and idioms. However, all grammar cannot be taught through substitution tables. It is not suitable for prose and poetry teaching. Moreover, this method will take a long time to formulate adequate linguistic habits.

6 TEACHING OF VOCABULARY

Teaching of English usually aims to develop the skills of understanding, speaking, reading and writing. Within each of the skills, attention must be given to phonology (the phonetic and phonemic system), to the grammar (the structure system), and to the vocabulary (the lexicon). Each of the language skills makes use of sounds, structure and vocabulary.

Within vocabulary (the lexicon of the language), we distinguish between content words (school, pen, etc.) and function words (with, for, may, will, etc.). The function words need to be learnt in a logical order and sequence. The content words can be learnt in small groups around life situations.

Although vocabulary is important, its prompt acquisition in the early stages should be subordinated to that of the sounds and the structure (grammar) of the language. Vocabulary can be accumulated as the need arises and as wider reading begins after the basic sound and structure system of the language has been learnt. Vocabulary items, low on a word-frequency list, should be taught as soon as feasible if such teaching stimulates students to talk about the immediate environment. For example, words like cow, dog, may have to be taught immediately if the classroom window looks out on them. The watchword here is 'judiciously.' Those items are to be taught if they give the students the feeling that they are talking about the real things in their environment. Words rarely exist by themselves. They are seldom used independently. They form part of a grammatical phrase or an idiomatic or conversational phrase. Thus, when we teach the oral use of grammar, we teach vocabulary at the same time.

When we teach conversation and put stress on pattern practice, we are simultaneously teaching vocabulary since conversational patterns extend in many directions and involve a continuous use of new vocabulary. When we study reading, using it as the basis for oral drill and conversation, we are practicing new vocabulary. In short, the techniques which we use to teach grammar, conversation and reading are used to teach new vocabulary. The method may be described as an inductive one. Emphasis is not placed directly upon the new vocabulary itself, but rather upon the grammatical or conversational phrase. Vocabulary is learnt in the context of the entire phrase. This does not exclude the consideration of other techniques which individual teachers may wish to employ. Some teachers use dictation regularly to implement the teaching of new words. They may also use conventional methods, such as putting new words on the blackboard at the end of each lesson and then drilling the students on these words in various forms. The teacher may ask questions using the new words, or he may require that students make up original sentences with the new words. The teacher may also assign the new words for study at home as part of the written assignment. The teacher may use any such technique which seems to give good results. He should abandon any technique which does not prove practical regardless of any professional recommendations it may carry.

There are ways in which the language-learner can be helped to understand the meaning of a word by using different approaches: (a) Demonstration - by showing an object or cut-out figure, by gestures, by performing an action, (b) Pictures - by using photographs, blackboard drawings, illustrations cut from magazines or newspapers, (c) Explanation - by description, by giving synonyms or opposites, by putting the word into a defining context, by translating. The language learner can be helped to connect the form of a word with its meaning by presenting the form and meaning together, so that the learner knows that they are connected to each other and this knowledge is firmly implanted in his automatic response. Unless there is some challenge the learner may not be interested enough to give his full attention and enthusiasm to the task of learning new vocabulary. The challenge and interest can be added to the teaching by: (1) making difficult for the learner to get the form of the word, i.e., the teacher forces the learner to guess, to follow the given clues, to search from previous knowledge; (2) making difficult for the learner to get the meaning of the word (3) making difficult for the learner to connect the meaning and the form. Thus the leaner must use his reasoning and interpretative abilities to find the answer. While using verbal explanations, the teacher can employ many techniques to introduce interest when teaching the form of the word. For example, he can write the meaning, using synonyms, opposites, a description, etc. However, it should not be so difficult for the learner that he gives up. Instead, it should help him towards a sense of achievement.

It must be kept in mind that the teaching of new vocabulary, like the teaching of any other phrase of language, is a difficult and complicated task. There are neither sure and easy ways of teaching new words nor are there any short-cuts to be taken. In teaching new vocabulary, the teacher should appeal to all the physical senses of the learner. The students should both hear and see the new words. The teacher should proceed pragmatically, making use of whatever teaching technique seems most logical at the moment.

Exercises related to word formation, synonyms and antonyms, and guessing the meaning of words from contexts are excellent means of increasing the vocabulary. Vocabulary should always be taught in normal speech utterances. New vocabulary items should be introduced in known structures. Vocabulary should be practiced as structures are practiced in substitution drills, transformation drills, questions and answers etc. Vocabulary items should be reintroduced many times with all the structures and in all the situations in which they can logically be used.

Students vary greatly in their responses to stimuli which will help them to remember vocabulary items. They should have the opportunity to repeat aloud and write new words as many times as possible. Like all aspects of the English language curriculum, vocabulary is integrated with other areas - speaking, reading and writing. Vocabulary can be developed with the students participating actively in the strategies listed below:

- Read, read, read: There is no better way to pick up words than by reading good books by authors who use language with precision and imagination.
- Have a good dictionary at home, which could be used to look up words and their roots, when coming across unfamiliar words.

- Keep a good pocket dictionary. which could be used to use the words in the right order when necessary.

The Communicative Approach:

In the 1970s and early 1980, English Language Teaching focusses on 'Communicative Competence'. Here language competence as seen as including

(a) Formal possibility, i.e., whether a sentence is possible grammatically.

(b) Feasibility, i.e., whether a sentence possible grammatically but hardly feasible.

(c) Appropriateness to context.

The ultimate aim in language learning is to acquire communicative competence: ability to say, listen, write and read.

The acquisition of linguistic skills doesnot seem to guarantee the consequent acquisition of communicative abilities in a language. On the contrary, it would seem that on overemphasis on drills and exercises for the production and reception of sentences tends to inhibit the development of communicative abilities. However, this is not to mean that such drills and exercises are not necessary. The abilities include the skills: one cannot acquire the former without acquiring the latter.

We need to remove the abilities from a dependence on linguistic skills in the mother-tongue and associate them with linguistic skills in the foreign language. Thereby we represent foreign language learning not as the acquisition of abilities which are new but as the transference of the abilities that have already been acquired into a different means of expression. If done successfully the learner can go on to extend the range of communication abilities through the foreign language without reference to his mother-tongue. Language Education must be concerned with the 'communicative competence' of the learner to be able to participate in a society as an able communicating member. It involves not just competence in the underlying linguistic system but also in language use, attitudes and beliefs about language and knowledge of the complex patterns of discourse used by the society. (Chomsky, 1965)

While Communicative Language Teaching remains the predominant approach within second and foreign language instruction, its limitations have become increasingly clear over the past decade of research in second language acquisition. Specifically the lack of emphasis on explicit grammar instruction, its primary focus on basic interpersonal communication and the limited relevance of its pedagogy for learners' academic and professional goals are the main objections to this communicative methodology.

New approaches have attempted to address these concerns while maintaining a communicative focus, emphasizing a highly interactive learning environment and increasingly providing a more authentic context for learning.

Communicative Language Teaching (CLT) educators have developed techniques to promote communicative use of the target language in the classroom. Task-based and project-based approaches (Nunan, 1989) to language learning have been suggested with the principles of promoting students authentic use of the target language for meaningful communication.

Firmly grounded in second language acquisition research, task-based activities engage learners in meaningful goal-oriented communication to solve problems, complete projects, etc.

The task-based syllabus abandons the formal specifications of language content. Instead, the syllabus is conceived as a sequence of tasks to be undertaken or problems to be solved, which have some meaningful, non-linguistic outcome. The foreign language elements, whether vocabulary or grammatical sentences are introduced and practised as necessary for the successful completion of the task.

The Constructivist Approach:

During the past several decades Educators have turned increasingly towards constructivist theories of language and learning, initially as a way to explain processes of child language development, and more recently as a framework for understanding school learning as well.

Constructivist approaches have become popular in education partly because they provide a powerful framework for thinking about teaching and learning. Rather than focussing either on specific content to be learned on or the nature of the learner, they lead to a consideration of learning in context : to how knowledge develops within a particular classroom. Such a framework provides a way to approach the problem of defining broad underlying principles that govern effective teaching and learning.

Conversation Analysis (CA) and talk-interaction in classrooms was originally established in sociology during the 1960s and since then it has found its way into various other disciplines including Applied Linguistics. CA's primary objective is describing the procedures and expectations, through which the participants accomplish orderly and intelligible social interaction. CA considers that it is not only that the physical context of classrooms may influence the ways in which the participants act the way they do, but also that the very ways in which the participants construct their interaction, based on their shared practices, creates the pedagogical context.

In the language classroom a number of educators have based on this framework to move on teaching, looking in more detail at the ways the structure of interaction within a particular context for learning shapes the knowledge and skills that learners develop, including their understanding of and ability to function within the social context itself.

Effective teaching and learning must allow room for learners to make their own contribution to ongoing task. They must establish their own purposes for what they are doing with language. For it is these purposes that integrate and give point to the specific skills and strategies they draw on as a task is carried out.

HPH

7 READING

Just as listening has as its goal the comprehension of the spoken language, the ultimate goal in reading is to comprehend the written language. The ability to decipher the spoken symbols (the sounds of the language) is paralleled in reading with the ability to decode the written symbols. Learning to read a second language is made easier if students already know how to read their first language, i.e., they have already learnt the process of relating graphic symbols to the language which they speak.

In reading, the major emphasis is on the identification of sound-symbol correspondences so that students perceive in graphic form, the meanings with which they have become familiar in oral form. Reading is an integrated part of language study, not a specialized activity. Reading helps the students to coordinate their eye movements, to link symbols they are accustomed to hearing (i.e., acoustic symbols) to those they see in print (i.e., visual symbols), to recognise grammatical units, to learn the spelling patterns which are basic to reading, and to grasp the full meaning of a statement through the signals and symbols (phonological, grammatical, and lexical) used in it.

(a) Reading is linked with listening. Students learn to segment an oral message (to identify its phrase structure groupings) and try to recognise these grouping in graphic form.

(b) Reading is linked with speaking. Students learn to say a few simple words in English and recognise the graphic symbols for the oral utterances they have been practicing.

(c) Reading is linked with improvement in pronunciation (including intonation). Students practice correct production of sounds and appropriate phrasing as they learn to associate symbols with sounds.

(d) Reading is linked with writing. Students consolidate sound symbol associations through dictation exercises. They confirm this learning by copying out with correct spelling, write out sentences as they practice reading.

(e) Reading is linked with the learning of grammar. Students see in written form what they have been learning and consolidate their grasp of grammatical structure.

(f) Reading is linked with learning about language. Students become conscious of the surface structure of the language, which are more clearly observable in written language.

(g) Reading is linked with learning about the culture of the speakers of the language. The written script in textbooks should be accompanied by illustrations and photographs, which elucidate many aspects of the life and customs of the people and add new meaning to the simplest of exchanges in the language, foreign to the learner.

What is reading? Reading is a process of looking at a written or printed symbol and translating it into an appropriate sound. Reading consists of 3 elements - the symbol, the sound and the sense.

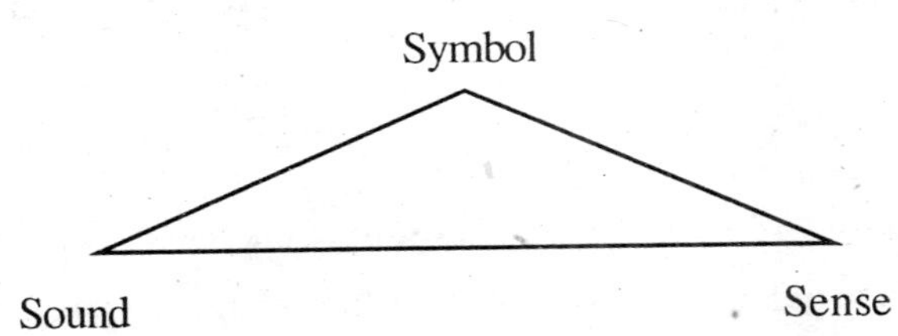

Reading is the 'ability' which enables the students to read with the purpose of extracting from the printed page, the thoughts, facts and information that has to give. By reading, we mean reading comprehensively. Reading for comprehension is a skill which can be developed by and by.

Aims of teaching reading:

(a) to recognise words,

(b) to understand the meaning of the words,

(c) to react to what has been read,

(d) to change ideas and behaviour of the students.

English is not a phonetic language. Its spelling system create problems in reading. So it is very essential that reading should be started after giving practice in listening and speaking.

Types of Reading: (i) Reading Aloud (ii) Silent Reading

(i) Reading Aloud

Means reading a book by producing sounds audible to others. This type of reading is useful during the first three or four years of language learning. Loud reading plays a very significant role in the teaching of language.

Reading aloud by the teacher can help the students towards the improvement of their listening ability. They are also able to share their recognition of different sounds. It also helps the learners to watch the movements of organs of speech of the teacher when he is presenting model reading to them. Some of the words which the students find difficult to speak are well understood by them. Pronunciation of the students is also improved considerably. Thus, reading aloud by the teacher helps the learners in a number of ways. The ultimate aim in reading aloud is reading with proper expression.

Objectives of Reading Aloud

The teaching of Reading aloud has three main objectives:

(a) To give practice in pronunciation, articulation, correct intonation, right emphasis, tone, speed, etc. Reading is a stage towards learning to speak English well. The words are provided so that the pupil does not have to think of the words he is going to read.

(b) To test the pupils knowledge of English words and phrases, and whether he knows how to pronounce them, how to phrase words, how to enunciate clearly. This reading aloud is a test as well as practice.

(c) To develop reading as an art so that pupils may learn to read aloud with proper expression and may learn, through their reading, to convey the feeling behind the words to their listeners.

The main aim is to make pupils realise the importance of making every word and syllable distinctly heard and understood by all so that it makes intelligible the meaning and significance of the general drift of the passage read.

Teaching of Reading Aloud

In reading aloud, attention should be given to posture and speed of the reader. Reading aloud can be greatly helped by good recitation work. Chorus reading should be discouraged, it may be done occasionally in lower classes to add variety to the lesson.

(ii) Silent Reading

Reading aloud is not the best training or preparation for thinking and assimilating the subject matter. So adequate attention should be given to pupils' silent reading and the teacher of English needs to devote a great deal of time and effort for this.

Silent Reading is useful at the advanced levels of learning a language. Reading aloud is only preparation for silent reading. At this stage, the learner has to read a number of books. At the higher stage, it is highly recommended that silent reading is both an end and a means of reading. It is a means to achieve the following objectives:

(a) **Intellectual:** Students are able to get out the facts or thoughts contained.

(b) **Literary:** Students get both enlightenment and entertainment.

(c) **Linguistic:** It aims at the expression of pupils' vocabulary.

All reading lessons should be preceded by plenty of oral discussion, in which difficult words, phrases and ideas should be explained by the teacher.

Intensive Reading

In dealing with the Intensive Reading in school, the pupil is required only to comprehend the lessons, but must learn to master the structures and vocabulary. This can be achieved through intensive reading. So intensive reading forms a very important aspect of learning a foreign language. In fact, language experts like Dr. West regards intensive reading as the most important activity of foreign language learning.

The intensive reading should be based on the structural syllabus containing interesting and well-graded reading material accompanied by colourful pictures to create an interest in the lessons. All reading lessons should be preceded by plenty of oral discussions in which difficult words, phrases and ideas should be clearly explained by the teacher. Lessons based on the intensive reader should have provision for both reading aloud and silent reading, to give the greatest benefit to a learner of English language.

Intensive, Extensive and Supplementary Reading

Intensive Reading means the detailed study of the passage. In this type of reading, the reader has to be very careful with different language items, i.e., words, grammar, language expression and ideas. He tries to understand everything contained in the paragraph.

In Extensive Reading, the reader is concerned with getting the overall meaning of the idea of the passage.

Generally, in lower classes, books are prescribed for intensive reading. But in higher classes, extensive reading, on the part of the student, is as important as intensive reading.

In intensive reading, student has to follow each word or structure contained in the paragraph. But in extensive reading, he can skip over a line or a word or structure which he fails to follow. Prescribed books in different classes are meant for intensive reading. Reading newspaper is meant for extensive reading.

In Indian schools, we find more stress being laid on intensive reading. The extensive reading is encouraged in a very few schools. Language-learner is expected to study a lot of material. So intensive reading should serve as a means to extensive reading.

Reading material for comprehension should be carefully structured and well graded. The passage for reading must be in accordance with mental level of the students. Simple, precise questions should be used for testing the comprehension of the students.

Teaching of Intensive Reading

Following steps are to be followed for conducting a prose lesson for comprehension:

(a) Introduction of the lesson.

(b) Model reading by the teacher.

(c) Practice in difficult language items, i.e., vocabulary and structures contained in the paragraph or lesson.

(d) Silent reading by the students (time limit should be prescribed).

(e) Comprehension questions concerning the lesson may be put. The questions should fit to the mental level of the learners.

(f) Application of the subject matter learnt.

Extensive Reading is based on SQ 3R Formula

S stands for Survey, Q for Questions, 3R stands for Read, Recite and Review.

Following are the steps for conducting a lesson on extensive reading:

(a) The Survey	Only very important words, extremely difficult one to be ignored.
(b) Questions	Pre-reading questions-answers to which they must look for while reading.
(c) More Survey	Teacher mentions main events, characters, ideas, etc.
(d) Reading	Students read the passage silently (they should be encouraged to read as quickly as possible).
(e) Recite Reproduction	After pre-reading questions are answered, other questions should be asked.
(f) More reviews	After satisfactory responses are given to the questions, teacher asks students to read the passage again silently. Teacher should set the time limit for silent reading; the increase in reading speed should be encouraged.

The main aim of extensive reading is to create an interest in reading for pleasure. Extensive reading should encourage the pupils to visualize what is read so as to make reading of prose a living experience. The primary objective of this reading is comprehension and not detailed language study. The main difference between intensive and extensive reading may be summed up as follows:

In intensive reading, a child learns to read, in extensive reading, a child practices what he has learnt. Broad questions for testing comprehension are generally planned as language exercise for extensive reading material.

A good scheme to encourage supplementary reading in class is to have many copies of two different books of similar difficulty and interest level to let half the class take home one set and the other to read the second set.

Methods of Teaching Reading

Reading should not be introduced to the students unless they have acquired the ability to speak the language. Children's first attempts at reading would be recognizing the shapes of letters. As soon as they are able to recognize the shapes, they should be taught to read the groups letters, i.e., words.

Look and Say Method: Reading is closely connected with the oral lesson. Pupil has to read only what he has learnt quite well through oral work. Teacher makes his pupils read words, phrases and small sentences from the blackboard which he writes while he is teaching. Teacher can make use of flash cards on which words similar in sound and spelling are written.

Walk, Talk, Chalk Method: Teacher holds up the cards one by one and pupils read Word Building Cards (cards showing endings of words like er, or, ar, ing, etc., are placed carefully). Selected words are written on the board. The class reads the words like holder, learner, shirting, etc.

Order Cards: Simple orders are written on cards or on a small roll up board and are flashed before the class for a few seconds. The pupils are told to read the order and follow it. No oral response is expected here. This gives training in quick reading and understanding. It is also a good test of reading with comprehension.

Picture Cards: Have a collection of small pictures cut out by pupils from magazines and newspapers. Write sentences on the class blackboard to suit the pictures. Ask pupils to supply pictures according to sentences after reading them. A good teacher must make use of many different methods and see that the procedure does not become rigid and dull.

Alphabetic Method: The students are taught the alphabets A, B, C. of the language. Here, the unit of teaching is a letter. Later, the students learn words by combining the alphabets. Here, too much emphasis is given on rote learning.

Phonic Method: Each word is broken up into basic speech sounds. The pupils are taught the different sounds first. They learn the alphabets afterwards. Here the teacher teaches English through the phonic script. It is a very common method in U.K. The only difficulty in its application is the need of expert teachers.

Word Method: Here the unit of teaching is a word. Pictures are also used with the words. The students look at the picture and say whatever they see. This method is also called Look and Say Method. It is very popular method of teaching reading. However, difficulty lies in its having pictures to be used for the words like 'to', 'of', 'at', 'from', 'in', etc.

Phrase Method: Here, the unit of teaching is a phrase. The students learn phrases and they learn the alphabets afterwards. The phrase method is based on the assumption that phrases are more interesting than words and place emphasis on the meaning. It is believed that since good readers recognize groups of words at each fixation of the eyes, the phrase method should foster rapid growth in efficient reading. However, this method cannot be used for all types of children because the weak students can hardly pick up one word at a time.

Sentence Method: Here, the unit of teaching is a sentence. Pupils learn words and alphabets afterwards. This method cannot be used for all types of children. It can be used when the children are exceptionally good in grasping.

Reading occupies a unique place today due to explosion of knowledge in every walk of life.

Aims of teaching reading:

(a) To give practice in the new words and sentence patterns done in oral lessons,

(b) To improve pupils' knowledge and command of the language,

(c) To train the mind systematically in absorbing ideas quickly and accurately from the printed page.

Teacher should set an example before the class as to how to read by his own model reading. Teacher's model reading should be followed by pupils' reading. Teacher should pay attention to the posture of the pupil while he is reading. Pupils should be given guidance as regards proper pronunciation, intonation and accent. Good reading and good speaking are interdependent. Good reading is a sure test of good understanding.

Teaching Pronunciation

Pronunciation is probably the most neglected aspect of English language teaching. English teachers often lack confidence to teach it methodically. As with English grammar, applied phonetics is rarely taught at school or even university, and therefore, seems an alien abstract subject to the adult trainee teacher.

The teaching of pronunciation should, however, be an integral part of the language course. For one thing, students are as concerned about pronunciation as they are with any aspect of learning English language.

Skilled pronunciation teaching also gives life to a class because it reflects feeling and personal reactions to different situations. In classroom practice, it gives variety to repetition or dialogues, which, otherwise, have only a neutral meaning.

One argument that the teacher has against pronunciation teaching is that it varies so much, depending on the situation and mood of the speaker, that it seems impossible to standardize anything. This argument, however, could also apply to grammar, as structure also depends on what the speaker is trying to say. Nevertheless, it is possible to make some attempt to break up English grammar into general rule and formulae. In the same way it is possible to lay down general guidelines for English pronunciation.

Static Forms: These consist of elements which have to be practised individually to ensure intelligibility.

Word Stress: Fortunately, the primary stress in most English words is on the first syllable:

Window, market, London, beautiful, manage, literal, country.

This also applies to genuine compounds: blackbird, post office, warlord.

Prefixes are not usually stressed: revolve, prepare, postpone, interfere.

With words of more than three syllables, the stress is often on the spoken syllable, that is third from the end:

Philosophy, laboratory, kilometre, psychological exceptions to this are usually words borrowed recently from other languages:

Guarantee, cigarette, magazine, hotel, address, shampoo, etc.

Sounds: It is important for a teacher to know how sounds are formed so that he understands when his students are doing wrong.

Consonants: The following classification of sounds follows from a description of what the mouth is doing when they are produced.

Bi-labial : When the lips are closed briefly to form consonant like 'p' in 'pet.'

Dental : When the tongue tip is placed against the teeth to form a consonant like 'th' in 'three.'

Alveolar : When the tongue tip touches the teeth ridge to form constants like ‘t' in 'time.'

Palatal : When the center of the tongue is raised towards the palate as with 'y' in 'yet.'

Velar : When the back of the tongue is raised towards the soft palate (or velum) as with 'k' in 'kick.'

Consonants vary depending on the place and movement of the tongue, or whether the voice is used, and, with some consonants, on positioning of the lips. From this comes various terms:

Voiced Voiceless : These describe whether the voice is used, (i.e., whether the vocal cords vibrate) as it is in 'v' in vine', or whether it is not, as in 'f in 'fine.' (Try saying 'f then 'v' with your finger over your vocal cords. You can feel the difference).

Plosive : Many consonants are formed by blocking the air stream and then releasing it suddenly, e.g., with the back of the tongue as in k/, g/, with the tongue tip as in 't', 'd', or with the lips as in 'p' and 'b'.

Fricative : This describes a sound produced through the friction of the air stream against partial obstructions in various parts of the mouth, as in 's' in 'slim' or 'th' in 'three.'

Nasal : This applies to consonants which are formed with the soft palate lowered so that the air stream passes through the nose: 'm' as in 'mat', 'n' as in 'not', and 'n' as in 'song'.

Several of these characteristics may be combined in a consonant like 'ch' as in 'chip', which is plosive and then fricative.

The interrelation between voice, or absence of voice, and the way the mouth is formed and moved, can be seen in the following example:

Consonant	Place	Manner	Voice
'f' far	labio dental	fricative	voiceless
'k' kick	velar	plosive	voiceless
'd' do	alveolar	plosive	voiced
'ng' song	velar	nasal	voiced
'y' yet	palatal	fricative	voiced

Awareness of this is useful as many mistakes made by learners are due to slight differences in sound production. One of the characteristics of India, as opposed to British English, is the tendency to curl the tongue tip for t and d. When your students make mistakes, it will help if you can analyse what you, yourself, are doing when you form consonants.

Vowels: Vowels are always voiced. They are formed in a less noticeable way than consonants, mainly by the position of the tongue and, secondarily, by the shape of the lips and movement of the jaw. Different vowels are determined by how high the tongue is raised in the mouth and by whether it is the front, middle or back part of the tongue which is being used.

English vowels are short or long, e.g., ship and sheep. The shape of the lips is also a determinant. Watch your mouth in a mirror and say 'ee', then change to 'o' as in robe, and 'oo' as in 'boot.' Notice how your lips become more rounded.

Diphthongs: Students of English tend to elongate or shorten diphthongs. Thus, Germans tend to extend the pronunciation of 'house,' as if it were 'haus' in their own language. In fact, dipthongs should take the same time to pronounce as long vowels, e.g., 'cow' and 'car' should take equally long to say. The French and some other languages have no diphthongs at all with the result that a Frenchman will shorten a diphthong and say 'wet' instead of 'wait.'

The Phonetic Alphabet: With beginners, it is worth introducing phonetics for different, difficult sounds or for sound-linking. The phonetic alphabet does simplify the relation between spoken and written English.

Symbols for Transcribing English Sounds:

Vowels		Diphthongs	
/i:/	bead	/ei/	bay
/i/	bid	/ai/	buy
/e/	bed	/oi/	boy
/ae/	bad		
/a	card		
/a/	cod		

Phonetics: Phonetics is that branch of linguistic science which deals with the study of speech sounds. Sounds of speech may be studied in two ways: from the point of view of (a) speaker and (b) listener. The speech sounds are formed by the adjustment and movement of certain muscles and the study of these adjustments and movements is called Motor Phonetics.

Advantages of Phonetics:

(a) By getting training in phonetics, we can arrive at an accurate and pleasing pronunciation of a foreign language.

(b) It is useful to modify speech habits or to establish new speech habits.

Every language has certain sounds, that are preculiar to that language, e.g., sound of English words are not produced in the same manner as the sounds of Hindi or French words. Thus each language has its own phonetics which explains how its sounds are produced and which is the correct manner of pronouncing them.

English phonetics and English spellings rarely coincide. Due to the presence of silent letter (palm), irregular spellings (write, right), etc. Hence, knowledge of phonetics is a great asset to a teacher of English in India.

English pronunciation is based on International Phonetic Alphabet, which was formulated in 1889 and on which most English dictionaries are formulated.

Phoneme : The smallest unit of sound which distinguishes one word from the other is called phoneme.

Speech sounds : English language has 26 letters of the Roman alphabet, but in standard English Speech there are 44 different sounds, which are known as phonemes; of these 12 are pure vowel sounds, 8 are diphthongs (diphthongs are combination of two vowel sounds, e.g., coin) and 24 are consonant sounds.

Proper articulation of consonant and vowel is important in pronouncing English words correctly. Apart from these, there are three other aspects of pronunciation that Indian speakers need to pay attention to. They are stress, rhythm and intonation.

Stress : The prominence of syllables in words or words in speech is called stress. Stress is not decoration to language but an important part of it. it makes the language clearly understandable. It is shown by a vertical stroke placed above the stressed syllable, for example, conduct.

Rhythm : It can never be talked about without referring to stress. It is simply the flow or the regularity of stress in a sentence. It is, in fact, a very significant characteristic of English speech.

Intonation : It is the term given to the rise and fall in the pitch of voice in speech. Change in pitch is due to the vocal chords. This difference in pitch creates difference in meaning. The real music of spoken English is found in intonation.

How to Teach Difficult Sounds?: Start with some sound which are already familiar to the learners. Only those sounds should be taken up first which are very near to the sounds already known. The steps could be summed up as follows:

I. Students produce the same sounds as done by the teacher.

II. Production of new sounds in words by the teacher.

III. Imitation by the students.

IV. Demonstration by the teacher showing the position of the various organs of speech.

V. Producing of sounds by the students.

VI. Testing State: Some minimal pairs will be prepared and written on blackboard. Teacher speaks the word one by one and the students tell the column from which it is spoken.

Remedial Programme for improving Pronunciation

Pronunciation Drills:

There are two types of Pronunciation Drills:

(a) Recognition Drill,

(b) Reproduction Drill.

While teaching sounds of English words, recognition drills may be taken up first, which should be followed by reproduction drills.

Recognition drills can be given in the following ways:

(a) By presenting minimal pairs: Minimal pairs are simply pairs of words that differ in one sound only: for example, bed, bad; hit, hid; ball, call; etc. Some minimal pairs are written by the teacher on blackboard in two different columns, for example,

A	B
Pin	pen
Tin	thin
Tree	three

Teacher speaks the words and the students are asked to tell the column out of which it is spoken. They will be able to say it correctly if they recognize the sound.

(b) By asking the students to carry out certain orders, e.g., sit at your seat, sit at his seat, etc.

(c) By asking students to give answers to certain questions: students are asked to identify sentences with the given meanings.

(d) By presenting pictures on charts or flash-cards: by showing them to students, the teacher speaks those words or sentences.

Students look at the picture, listen to the teacher and try to read recognizing the sounds. This type of read and listen exercises help the learners considerably. Thus the students learn the recognition of sounds first and then they are enabled to produce the sounds themselves. This way of reaching the sounds of words is called Reproduction drills.

(a) Teacher takes up a minimal pairs of words. He speaks the word or words and the students repeat after him. This type of drill work can also be taken up by using the minimal pairs in sentences, for example:

I want a pen

I want a pin.

(b) Model dialogues, Substitution Tables, and reading passages are built around the problem sounds. Thus the students get practice of producing these sounds.

(c) Oral compositions are built around problem sounds.

(d) Some of the songs and simple poems may be selected for further oral practice.

Pronunciation is mostly learnt through imitation and so it is essential that the teacher should have a model type of spoken English. Teacher of English language should learn stress, rhythm and intonation before teaching pronunciation.

Teacher of English language should be able to compare the sounds of English with the sounds of mother tongue. That way, the students pick up English sounds more correctly. Their liability of speaking English like mother tongue is also got rid of. Certain features of English which are not present in mother tongue should be emphasized. As far as possible, a good deal of practice should be given to the learners and their attention must be drawn to the peculiarities of English language.

Pronunciation Charts

The most commonly known kind of pronunciation chart is the articulation diagram (Fig.1). This is usually a number of drawings showing the positions of the organs of speech during the production of a significant sound. The names and functions of each of the speech should be introduced first. Later, let your students know the position of these organs while pronouncing vowel, consonants, and other features of speech. If the students can pronounce a certain sound correctly, there is no need to explain some sounds, charts may help in improving their pronunciation.

Pronunciation charts (wall-size ones, Fig. 1.) and articulations diagrams, may help in recognizing the students' mistakes and which changes in the position of speech organs are necessary in order to correct wrong pronunciation. By looking at diagrams, learners have means by which they realize what is going on in their mouths while sounds are produced. In teachers' training programmes, diagrams are necessary because they show how each sound is named according to the nature and positions of speech organs used in producing it. The teacher trainers can therefore pronounce these sounds according to their description in some teachers manuals.

The following general recommendations for the presentation of articulation diagrams and their use to the teacher and students should be followed:

(a) While presenting the production of a certain sound, avoid very technical terms. The tip of the tongue, the ridge of the teeth and the Adam's apple are preferable.

For Improving Pronunciation:

(a) Drills may be given with the teacher's model pronunciation. Audio aids like record players, tape recorders, can be used for this purpose.

(b) Minimal pairs of words may be found (pairs of words that differ in sound only e.g., bad, bed, pen, pin, hit, hid), with the help of which, teacher can teach as well as test pupils pronunciation.

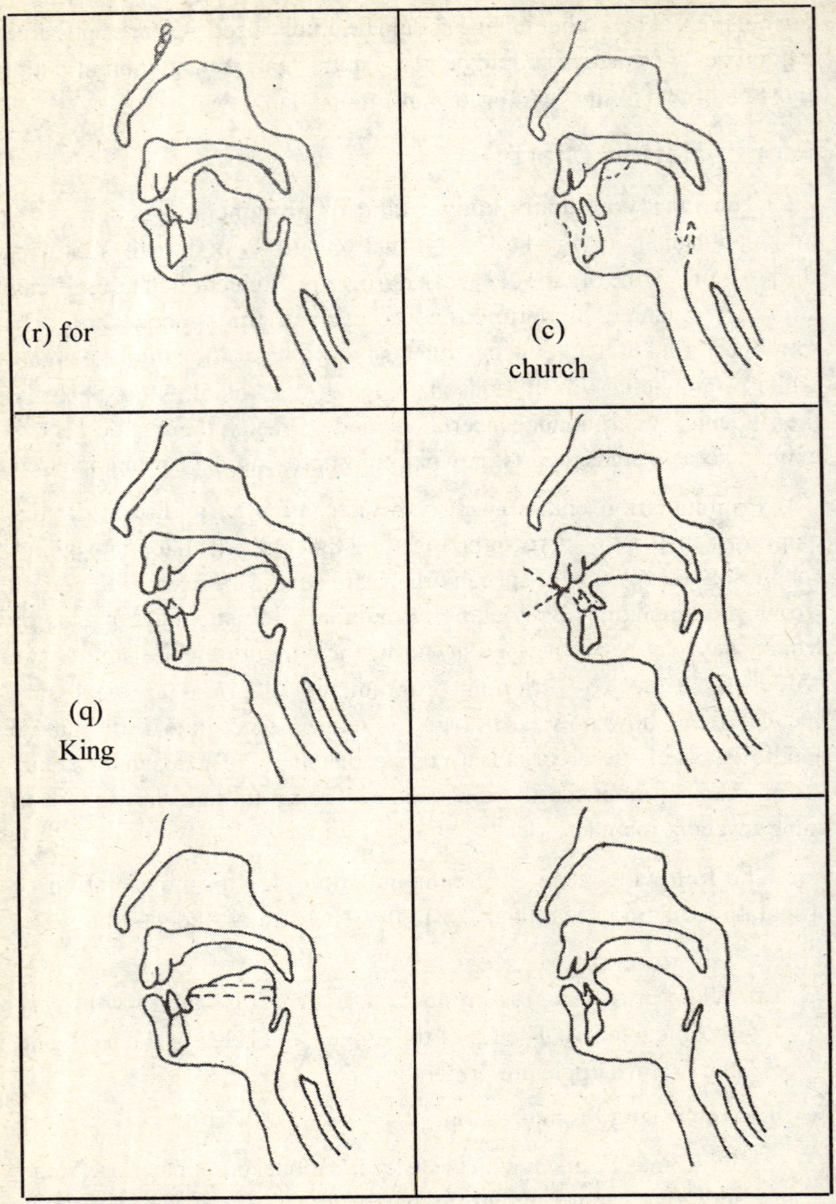

Fig. 1. Pronunciation Chart

(c) Listening to BBC News from radio, television.

(d) Referring to English pronouncing dictionaries like (i) English Pronouncing Dictionary by David Jones and (ii) The Advanced Learner's Dictionary of Current English by Hornby, Gatenby, and Wakefield.

Where competent teachers are available, systematic training of the ear, supplemented by gramophone, tape-recorder and radio can go a long way towards improving the pronunciation of the learners.

Reading aloud, both by the teacher and students, help towards improving the pronunciation of the words. Before reading aloud, the teacher should select some of the words contained in the passage, which are likely to be mispronounced by the students. The teacher should drill the sounds, stress patterns and intonation patterns. Then the teacher's reading of the passage should be carried out, following which the brighter students should be asked to read the paragraph. In this way, the weak students get more chances of listening to correct pronunciation. In the words of A.W. Fairly, 'It gives practice in the manipulation of sounds and practice in speech and pronunciation.'

The development of reading activities will help learners reinforce listening and speaking abilities. In regular teaching programmes, reading and writing can well serve as a starting point for extensive listening-speaking activities. Moreover, interesting reading experiences will provide topics for oral discussion and for writing. The introduction of reading places a great responsibility on the teacher since reading presupposes two quite different sub-skills. Teacher helps students (a) bring meaning of connected discourse (b) get meaning from the printed or written material. Moreover, students should be motivated to continued reading out of class. Reading should be inculcated as a pleasant hobby. People read for many practical or recreational purposes. To ensure detailed comprehension of the passage, the reading material should be read aloud by the teacher - pausing normally at logical points within the sentences to indicate the relationships of linguistic items - as the students follow in their textbooks. Reading means looking at written material.

To develop reading skills:

(a) Motivate the reading by relating it to the students experiences or in the case of a longer story, essay, or chapter which is begun, by eliciting a brief summary of what has been read.

(b) State the purpose of the reading.

(c) Clarify the situations so that students can understand the major purpose of the passage.

(d) Extend and enrich the experiences of students so that they will understand the elements in the situation (people, place, time, and cultural allusions).

(e) Present the sounds and meanings of unfamiliar vocabulary along with the sound-symbol correspondences.

(f) Help students to read words in logical groups.

(g) Help learners understand the grammatical function of structures and word-groups.

(h) Enable the readers to distinguish between the main theme and supporting details.

(i) Increase their speed in reading, since slow, laboured reading decreases comprehension.

8 TEACHING OF PROSE

Pupils should be trained to read books, not bits of books. But if books of extracts are used, they should be of passages which will serve as fitting introductions to the books from which they are taken.

Reading is one of the four fundamental skills of language-learning, which is best acquired through the teaching of prose. The immediate aim of teaching prose is:

(a) To strengthen the vocabulary and the sentence-patterns learnt in earlier lessons,

(b) To train the pupils in the use of new words and sentence patterns,

(c) To help the pupils acquire knowledge and command of all active vocabulary and

(d) To help the pupils follow the passive or recognition vocabulary.

The main objective of teaching prose lessons is to enable the pupils to master the structural items and content words. The objectives could be summed up as follows:

(a) To enable the pupils to master and reinforce the structural items,

(b) To enable the pupils to acquire the new vocabulary and content words,

(c) To develop the pupils power of comprehension through listening and reading,

(d) To enable the pupils to acquire the information contained in the lesson,

(e) To develop the ability of speaking English correctly and fluently.

In the textbook, there are various types of prose lessons. There are stories, essays, descriptives, biographies, plays, and letters. The specific objectives will differ from lesson to lesson.

Each prose lesson contains specific structural items and a number of new words. The four methods of teaching new words:

(a) By direct association of the word with the object, picture or model,

(b) By translation in the mother-tongue,

(c) By giving an equivalent definition or explanation in English,

(d) By using it in a suitable context and thus making it self-explanatory.

Explaining the most important key words from a lesson in the introduction stage would make the teaching of prose lesson smooth and enjoyable as there would not be any barrier towards the path of reading and understanding. After introducing the new words, the teacher should give a model reading of the lesson and then assign some portion for silent reading with some objectives in mind. Silent reading should be tested by the detailed questions afterwards.

Methods to Teach Structural Items

Teacher should proceed and present the structure in a systematic way. First, he should revise the necessary structures taught earlier and then he should proceed by creating a suitable situation to provide effective learning experiences. Effective teaching aids should be used to create a meaningful situation. The structures must be used by the teacher in his own sentences and the sentences should be repeated at least thrice. Teacher should write the sentences on the blackboard and undertake drilling of the sentences. When he is sure that the pupils have mastered the structures, the teacher might ask suitable questions based on the items. Later, the pupils are made to copy the blackboard writing and the structural items are further reinforced with the help of substitution table. The steps of teaching may be summed up as follows:

(a) Teacher's model reading,

(b) Purposeful repetition and drills.

(c) **Blackboard work:** All new content words and phrases should be written by the teacher on the Blackboard.

(d) **Summary:** Contents are learnt in small bits of information. All these can be organised to provide a complete verbal picture of the unit.

Teachers should evaluate the learning outcomes in the light of objectives set in view. The prose lessons are meant for detailed study of the text and the main aim is acquiring mastery over the language. So, there should be questions with the textual matter designed to test the comprehension of the lesson by the pupils. The teacher can recapitulate the teaching unit by way of asking some broad general questions. This would be followed by giving a variety of exercises like using new words in sentences of their own, filling in the gaps with appropriate words, writing the answers of some thought-provoking questions, etc. In this way the teaching of prose would help in achieving objectives like cultivating the habit of attentive perceptive reading, developing the ability of extracting the significant and meaningful matter from the text and developing interest in further reading by making reading easier for learners.

HPH

9 TEACHING OF POETRY

Experience teaches that poetry is a delight accessible to almost all. The poet writes a poem to express objectively and achieve catharsis through a strongly felt emotion. The poem is similar to the pearl created in the oyster shell as a result of an irritation or disturbance; but it is not only a creation in its own right, it normally embodies on objective picture or reproduction of the event.

Poetry moves in a different dimension from that of prose. We can compare prose to walking, poetry may be compared then to dancing, rising above the surface of the earth, perceiving its relations, getting a fuller view of its reality. If we bring our pupils continuously and systematically to a vital and fully conscious experience of the best poetry, that is within their reach, we are giving them a means of emotional expression, and of emotional and aesthetic perception, in that state of heightened awareness, that is generated by rhythm and pattern in sound. Poetry is more memorable than prose. The formal arrangement of the rhyme and rhythm — the pattern — make it easier to memorise and to hold in the memory than unpatterned prose.

Poetry is to be presented through speech. Poetry, like all other language material, must be introduced orally with the books closed and nothing to distract the attention from or compete with the poem through the eye. We may make three simple rules in poetry teaching:

(i) Too much explanation should be avoided. MacLeish's stricture that poems 'should not mean, but be' has become a cannon for poetry teaching.

(ii) Verbal peculiarities should be passed over. Such forms as hath, doth, yon, thou and thee, should be ignored altogether.

(iii) Good art can be allowed to make its own impact. Most good art makes its own impact directly on the emotions and the subconscious mind.

Poetry is a thing of beauty because it has beauty of language, beauty of form, beauty of thoughts and beauty of emotion. Coleridge once defined prose as 'words in their best order' and poetry as 'the best words in their best order.'

Poetry develops the child's sensitiveness to beauty, especially beauty of language and thought and helps to develop his imagination. So the main aim of teaching poetry is to help our students appreciate and enjoy poems. The purpose of poetry teaching is to develop the aesthetic sense of the pupils and appreciation of the beautiful. Appreciation of poetry is an experience. It is the teacher's duty to arouse pupils' interest and awareness to this living experience.

Poetry gives enjoyment. Its main aim is to give pleasure. It has direct appeal to the heart. Poetry opens up a new world before the pupils, which is filled with beauty, charm, imagination and wonder. The rhythm of poetry helps the children to acquire a natural speech rhythm for speaking English. This is specially true at the early stage of poetry-reading.

Poetry is beauty — beauty of form, language, thoughts, moods and feelings. It is the teacher's role to bring the child's awareness and insight into this beauty. Poetry can be caught, it cannot be taught. Teacher must make the poetry live through his teaching. Poetry should be taught for enjoyment of thought, feeling, imagery and rhythm. If the teacher is not moved by the emotion of the poem, he cannot inspire his pupils. Poetry is not read like prose, it is rather recited. Reciting the poetry well is worth more than all explanations, meanings and paraphrasing that can be given. As far as possible, poetry should be taught as a whole. It should be appreciated as a total work of art.

Objectives of Teaching Poetry at Different Levels of School Curriculum

(a) To help pupils appreciate the beauty of thought,

(b) To help develop pupils imagination,

(c) To help pupils develop the aesthetic appreciation of the poem.

Methods of Introducing Poems to the Pupils

To help develop the appreciation of the beautiful, poetry should be introduced to the pupils in an appropriate manner. The various methods of introducing poems could be summed up as follows:

(a) Biographical Method: Introducing the poet and his life-sketch before reading the poem. This method is appropriate when the children know something about the poet to be interested in the poem.

(b) Explanatory Method: The poem is introduced by giving the gist of the poem in the beginning. Jotting of difficult words on blackboard may also be done in higher classes.

(c) Synthetic Method: The teacher draws out the whole poem for the children by skilful questioning which involves an active participation of the pupils. The teacher must read the poem while children listen and try to catch the rhythm and spirit of the poem.

Alexander Hadow states that there is no set method for teaching poetry. Poetry is beauty and beauty is truth. To be an effective poetry teacher, all that teacher needs is to love poetry and then the method is teacher's own. The desired learning outcome is to make the children feel the beautiful, love the beautiful and to deepen that love through the appreciation of the poem.

Methods of Teaching Poems at Different Levels of the School

The primary appeal of the poetry is to the ear.

(i) Song-Action Method (for lower level): At early stage, the rhythm of poetry helps the children to acquire a natural speech rhythm for speaking English. So the teacher's sing-a-song rhythm of the poetry reading with appropriate gesture and action makes the pupils enjoy the poetry immensely.

(ii) **Discussion Method:** This method aims at testing the comprehension of the poem. The discussion stage is designed to lead to a deeper all-round perception of the poem.

(iii) **Appreciation Method:** Poet Coleridge has described poem as 'the best words in the best order.' Accordingly, the aim of the method is to enable the pupils to appreciate the beauty of language and thought and to refine their emotions.

To sum up, in the process of teaching a poem, three main stages could be seen as follows:

(i) **Preparation:** Equipping the pupils with the main outline of the poem by familiarising the most important words and expression and ensuring that the ideas involved are not beyond their reach.

(ii) **Presentation:** Reading, including a great deal of re-reading, and calling for intense concentration on the words of the poem. Books are not to be opened until the poem has been made thoroughly familiar to the ear and there is likely to be no conflict between what is imagined in the ear as it is read and the printed words when they are read.

(iii) **Discussion:** Based on a thorough knowledge of the text of the poem, it is designed to lead to a deeper perception of the poem the ideas it embodies, and to expression.

The aim of teaching poetry is not language or word study: it is to understand and appreciate the language, style and mood of the poet, his way of expressing things. It is to develop in our pupils an aesthetic sense and appreciation for better things and to create an eye for the beautiful.

Why Teach Poetry?

There are three main grounds on which we may justify time being spent on teaching poetry in school hours.

(a) Reading poetry is a joy in itself. It is a direct awareness of sights, sounds and events. A delight in poetry-reading educates the width and depth of our response to life. It is one of the most potent of all enduring influences.

(b) Poetry, like all the arts, makes its appeal to the mind. It nourishes the imagination and through that, the very root of mental life.

(c) Poetry provides some form of training of personality which enhances a man's moral judgement. Moral judgements are essentially judgements of what is or what is not — a noble line of action for a man to take.

Poetry, truly appreciated, nourishes the roots of mental life. Imagination is a primary quality of mind. The more imaginatively aware a child is, the more material does he come to possess into the making of his life. Imagination and its near relative — intuition — are the qualities (underrated) by most teachers and perhaps by the civilization to which we belong. Modern educational systems emphasize discipline, common sense, possession of knowledge and the power to manipulate the facts acquired. The outcome is training man to think without encouraging their power to experience and to imagine.

A school curriculum weighed against poetic and artistic appreciation, tends to encourage looking at things from the outside. A child is taught to observe the leaves of a tree at the expense of delighting in the fact that they are leaves. He is taught to analyse the rational meaning of sentences rather than to understand their non-rational implications.

Delight in poetry necessitates a certain healthy detachment from the tyranny of 'here' and 'now.' A good poetry is a powerful antidote against self-deception of sentimentality in any of its myriad forms.

In the high school years, the primary aim of poetry-reading should be pleasure: delight in sound, in rhythm and meter, in shared emotional experience, in the varied forms of verse. The student should encounter poems, which present a rhythmic story to quicken his pulses, a lyric moment to touch his emotions or a series of visual images sketched in graphic words.

Poetry develops the child's sensitiveness to beauty, specially beauty of language and thought and helps pupils to develop the imagination. The chief aim of teaching poetry is to help pupils appreciate and enjoy poems.

Poetry opens up a new world before the pupils which is filled with beauty, charm, imagination and wonder. The rhythm of poetry helps acquire a natural speech rhythm. This is specially true at the early stage of learning the language. To succeed in teaching poetry, teacher must himself love poetry, love it with his eyes open. He must be able to read a poem aloud as if he loved it and was absorbed by it. If he fails to suggest that he cares for the poem, then he can hardly expect his pupils to care for the poem. Teaching a poem is an art. While teaching poem, the teacher should become one with the feelings of the poet, be able to create proper atmosphere for the poem.

Principles of teaching a poem:

(a) Model recitation of the teacher at the beginning of teaching is essential because it helps in creating an appeal to the students towards the poem.

(b) Detailed explanation of the lines of the poem should be avoided.

(c) Verbal peculiarities of the language of the verse should, as far as possible, be avoided.

(d) As far as possible, poem should be taught as a whole. It should be approached as a total work of art.

The total effect should be a memorable lesson, an increased respect for the poet as maker, and a greater liking for poetry.

Appreciation of Poetry

The appreciation of poetry involves an awareness of rhythm and there is good reason to believe that such awareness may be a powerful factor in coordinating the working of body and mind.

Poetry supplies children with an aesthetic experience and can be used from the early stage. Most teachers, however, seem to think that poetry should not be taught to the beginners until they have a sufficient command of the language. If, however, they attempt to teach a poem they often make the mistake of trying to explain every word in it, thus hampering real appreciation. The teacher need not hesitate to introduce poetry at a comparatively early stage. The teacher can make use of poetry records for this purpose in following ways:

(a) Giving a short introductory talk containing the main points in the poem,

(b) The pupils listening to the recording of the poem more than once,

(c) The pupils select the poem they like best by listening to several recordings,

(d) The selected poems are played in the 'listeners' request programme,' which can be held once a week or so,

(e) The pupils select portions of the poem for reading aloud,

(f) The teacher helps the pupils learn any poem by heart if they wish so by writing out the poem on the blackboard.

For the purpose of creative composition of the poem, Poetry Workshop conducted twice a year would be useful. The teacher may invite local English poets as resource persons for the workshop. Workshops of this kind will go a long way towards the appreciation of poem and thereby the appreciation of the beauty of the words and sound of the language.

HPH

10 TEACHING OF GRAMMAR

It is now generally acknowledged that language learning is not simply a mechanical process of habit-formation, but a process which involves the active cooperation of the learner as a rational individual. Far from being the passive recipients of stimuli in the form of exercises and drills, students learn in a selective manner, searching for the information they need, to discover the system of the language being learnt.

A grammar is a system that describes how the language works – its sounds, word-forms and word-groups. Structural linguists stressed the language of speech as primary, with the written language as a derivative. Through 'pattern practice' and 'substitution drills' they have encouraged students to imitate the observed linguistic behaviour. Grammarians describe the structural features of language. A modern grammarian is interested in describing language, not prescribing it.

Most teachers continue to see language learning as fundamentally an inductive process based on the presentation of data, which can be controlled by explanations of a suitable type. Knowledge of grammatical theory is an indispensable part of every language teacher's training which calls for some explicit description of the grammar as an essential element in both first and second language teaching. It is believed that in any given classroom situation, just as much attention should be given to grammar as may be necessary in order to promote efficient language learning. The teaching of grammar is seen not as an end in itself, but as a useful aid in helping students to achieve the practical mastery of a language.

The study of grammar, laying stress on the elementary structures of the language, is as essential as the study of vocabulary, pronunciation, reading, and any other phase of language. It provides a basis upon which the language-learning can be built. Without the guidance of grammar, the student is adrift on a vast sea of complex language forms which would make little sense to him. Functional grammar serves to reduce these forms to set patterns. The student studies these patterns and learns to master them. In this way he is able to increase his understanding and use of the language. Mr. I. Morris, the British writer in the field of language teaching, after surveying the whole area of argument for and against grammar teaching, concludes: (a) a consideration of grammar in language-learning is imperative; (b) a systematic language course calls for grammatical progression concurrent with vocabulary progression.

English language has three essential characteristics. They are as follows:

(1) The word-order and the sentence patterns,

(2) The structural words, and

(3) A few inflections.

The study of the functions of these three essentials of the language constitutes the study of grammar. The parts of speech enable us to distinguish the different kinds of functions that different words do. The names of the parts of speech like nouns, pronouns, adjectives are nothing but the names for those different functions.

The aim of a grammar lesson, in early stages, is to create an interest in words, to sharpen sensitivity to their spirit and use. Learning a language demands learning to be sensitive to language in general, learning to be alert to language signals. Grammar is the analysis of the structure of the language - 'its anatomy.' The teaching of grammar is justified as a means to an end. The end is clear expression, the ability to express what one wishes to communicate so that the receiver (listener or reader) can take it in without undue effort and without being misled or confused. The teaching of grammar helps in the formation of correct language habits. Hence, it should largely be carried on through the examples by use of model sentences and numerous examples, through the use of the Direct Method, through construction exercises such as sentence completion, etc., and also through intensive questions and answers. Grammar must always follow language. It must never precede it.

Objective of Teaching Grammar

Grammar is the science of language. Teaching of Grammar undertakes a scientific study of a language, analyses it into its components and presents certain facts arranged under some general categories, e.g., subject and predicate, nouns, pronouns, verbs, etc.

Grammar is taught to study the behaviour of words — changes in the word forms.

Grammar is taught to let pupils understand the sentences spoken and written, e.g., the difference between 'Raj has given a toy' and 'Raj was given a toy.' Pupils should be able to speak grammatically correct sentences. The communication activities require the use of acceptable English which results from the knowledge of Grammar. Teaching of Grammar is a means whereby faulty speech and composition are corrected.

Grammar needn't mean pedantry, routine for routine's sake; it can mean a valuable necessary discipline, or even a fascinating study. Grammar resembles a vitamin in that ill effects may spring from a deficiency and an excessive dosage may be wasteful and harmful.

Formal Grammar and Functional Grammar

Formal grammar is that grammar which is taught in a formal way. It is also called the prescriptive grammar or the traditional grammar which deals with the definitions and rules of the language. In this type of grammar, there are set rules. The students first learn the rules and then practice the rules in speech and writing. The grammatical rule is looked upon as an authoritative law imposed by linguistic principles

Functional grammar is also called incidental grammar. This type of grammar is learnt by the students while learning the language. Here language-learning is the first concern of the learner and knowing the rules and regulations is the secondary concern. This type of grammar takes into account that language is growing and changing from time to time. It deals with the ability to use the language grammatically, i.e., an acceptable form of words, pattern of phrases, sentences, sounds, stress, rhythm, intonation, etc. It is the Grammar in operation.

Formal Grammar develops the ability to describe the language whereas Functional Grammar develops the ability to use the language: People learn Functional grammar when they are learning to speak the language.

Prescriptive and Descriptive Grammar

The grammatical rule, looked upon as an authoritative law, imposed by grammatical principles, gives rise to Prescriptive Grammar.

Another approach to look upon a grammatical rule is to consider it to be a generalised statement of usage. This grammar tells us how language should be used, that is, it describes the use of language.

Language is a living thing — it grows and develops, it recognises different usages for formal and informal speech and writing. Grammar describes how words work together in a sentence, i.e., the various ways in which they are related to each other and the part that each plays in expressing meaning.

Methods of Teaching Grammar

Language is a means of communication. To facilitate better and accurate communication, every language must follow certain rules and regulations. When words change, their forms to show change in time we get tenses. Similarly we learn about 'Singular' and 'Plural' which show changes in number. Teaching of Grammar helps the language learner to be alert to language signals. So that the utmost economy in time and effort is assured to the learner, there must be rigorous organisation of the language course on a skeleton of grammar, of which the language teacher must be fully conscious throughout.

(I) Deductive Method: Deductive method of teaching grammar starts with the general rule, e.g., definition of Noun. Then the general rule, e.g., the definition of Noun is applied to particular cases, i.e., by giving examples of Noun to clarify the general rule or the implications of the formula.

This method is easy for the teacher to teach but has been criticised by the linguists on the ground that the mental faculties of the pupils are not fully exploited while teaching Grammar. The power of thinking is not put to test and use.

(II) Inductive Method: Inductive method of teaching grammar starts with the examples based on the previous knowledge of the pupils. They are asked to analyse the examples, i.e., to find out the similar characteristics of the examples. This is the process of observation. Then they are asked to form an appropriate rule or definition with the help of which they are guided to arrive at a generalisation.

The Inductive method is a psychologically sound method. It makes pupils put in their efforts and apply their intelligence while learning the rules of the language.

However, the teachers should bear in mind that the Inductive method should be followed by the Deductive method. The Inductive method makes the pupils form the rule but the Deductive method can test and see whether they have grasped the rule. The two methods are complementary to each other.

The teaching of grammar should largely be carried on through the ample use of model sentences and numerous examples through the use of the Direct Method, through construction exercises, such as Sentence-Completion and similar exercises and also through intensive questions and answers. The main point to remember is that it is not the grammar of English that is difficult; it is English usage. Therefore explanation can do little, whereas practice can do much. The greater part of the learning should not be listening to explanations by the teacher, but applying what has been learnt by rote or analogy or observation.

The teaching of grammar fell into some disrepute during the period when the 'direct method' of teaching language was first introduced. The direct method was widely acclaimed as a great step forward in foreign language teaching. The direct method is not, strictly speaking, a method of foreign language teaching. It is, rather a principle, which can operate through various possible methods. The direct method was a definite step forward in the sense that it served to draw attention to the importance of using the English language orally in class. But the classroom is not the home, and the conditions of the classroom are in no way comparable to those of the home. The classroom, on the other hand, is a highly conventional situation. It exists for the only purpose of giving students concentrated and intensified experience in the field of learning. Time, also, is an important factor here. The only contact which most Indian students have, with the English language, is in the classroom. The course, therefore, should be carefully organised and the teaching methods, consistent with these facts, should be employed. The mature school-child's mind, unlike the child picking up his own mother tongue, is capable of observation and analysis; which is to be taken into consideration while teaching English.

In the literature of foreign language teaching, one comes across a great deal about inductive and deductive methods of teaching. 'Induction' means a process of learning or teaching whereby numerous examples of certain principle are presented and the rule is then inferred from these examples. 'Deduction' means starting with the rule and then offering examples to show how the rule applies. In direct method of teaching the language, where grammar is not formally taught, great emphasis is placed upon the inductive method of learning. It is assumed that, just as the child learns his tenses without formal study, the mature school-going child will come to understand and use these tenses correctly through more exposure to the language. The child has his entire childhood in which to learn his native language, whereas the English language student has only a few lessons in class each week. It is rare for an English language learner to get enough practice through mere class-work. Numerous examples may be given, and the student may even fail to see any relationship between these examples. It seems simpler and wiser, under these circumstances, to explain the rule first and then to give the examples later. Once a learner understands what he is doing and what he is supposed to learn, it is much easier for both him and the teacher to proceed.

In teaching functional grammar, reading material may be presented first. This material should contain examples that illustrate the new grammar rule to be studied. The reading material would be followed by a statement of the rule, followed by practice exercises. This would constitute an inductive approach. Deductive approach, on the other hand, would start with the grammar rule, followed by practice exercises, and then proceed to reading material where the grammar rule is applied in practical form.

It might be convincingly argued that at the elementary level, a degree of attention should be paid to structural considerations of the language, that cannot easily be given within the framework of a functional syllabus.

A grammatical approach at the lower levels, followed by a functional approach for more advanced levels, may prove to be the optimum solution. The student would thereby progress from learning how the language operates to learning how it is used; using both grammatical and functional syllabus respectively, to focus on each task.

The real task in the teaching of grammar is to give the learner sufficient oral practice with the rule so that he can make some practical use of it in understanding and speaking English. Teacher plays an important role here by providing oral practice, controlling it, and directing it towards the proper end. Knowledge of the grammatical rule constitutes merely a beginning. It is the drill work which follows, that serves to implant the rule in the student's mind for practical application. As the learner attains some fluency, the rules of grammar tend to disappear. But the practical forms remain. The correct forms begin to sound right to the ear. When the correct forms of the language begin to sound right, then the learner is on his way to learning the language.

HPH

11 TEACHING OF WRITING

Writing

The fourth and last of the communication skills is to help develop in our students is writing. Progressively, and in small steps, students should be taught:

(a) The sound-spelling correspondences,

(b) The mechanics of writing (punctuation, capitalization, spelling).

Writing has been characterized as written thinking. Language-learners should be encouraged to express their ideas, experiences, thoughts and feelings through writing. Any writing, free, controlled or creative, should have a content in harmony with their evolving interest. There are two major types of writing : practical and creative. Practical writing is found in letters as well as summaries, essays. Many of the learners will never write 'creatively,' but creativity, where observed, should be encouraged and carefully nurtured.

Basic Principles in Teaching Writing

The teaching of writing English must be viewed in two lights: First, it is a problem of assembling words to form grammatical sentences. Second, it is a rhetorical problem — a problem of teaching students to organise words and patterns so as to fulfill a given rhetorical aim. 'Rhetoric' implies the organisation of both form and content to meet a particular rhetorical aim, such as persuading a friend to take a certain course of action, or complaining to a neighbour about something. Writing any type of composition involves a number of complicated rhetorical and linguistic operations, which are to be broken down and taught separately. Students should be presented with tasks that they can successfully complete. The following diagram shows what writers have to deal with as they produce a piece of writing:

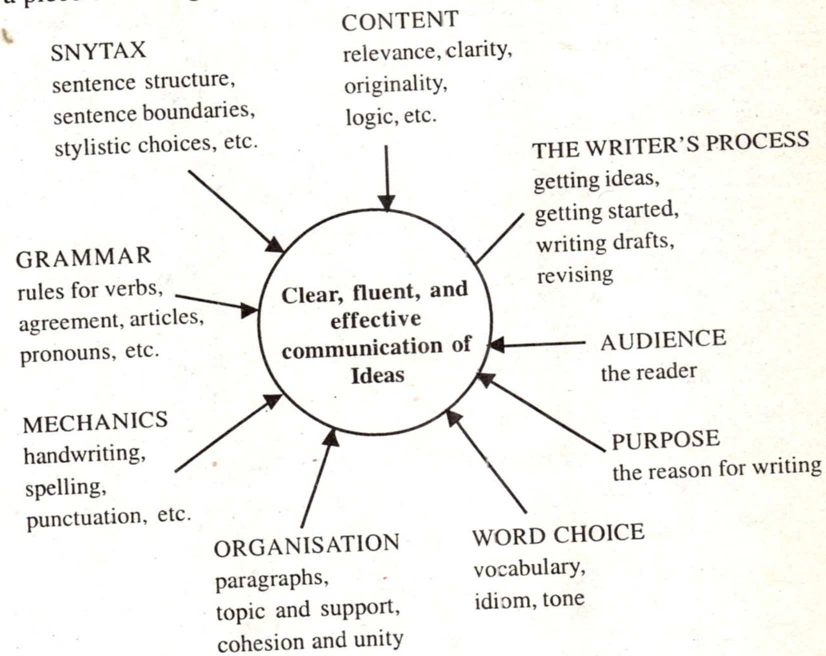

Fig. 2. Communication of Ideas

The different features of the diagram above, have resulted in the development of a variety of approaches to the teaching of writing.

Integrating Reading and Writing

When we write, we also read. Indeed, it is necessary to do so, since the process of creating a piece of written discourse depends on reading. Even before we write, we often read for information, which is subsequently to be incorporated in writing composition. In addition, the form and style of the composition itself will be shaped by the characteristics of the reader. So the process of writing depends reading before, during, and after the act of creating, and the writer who takes no account of the fact that he is writing for someone to read, runs the risk of producing something, which is unreadable. Given the complementarity of reading and writing, it is sensible to emphasise on the integration of these two skills in teaching pupils to write. There are a number of advantages to be derived from doing this. Firstly, the reading material can provide an example of the type of material which the students themselves should produce. What it implies is that student has an example of a piece of communication consisting of sentences that are grammatically connected and logically linked. Secondly, the reading material can be drawn from the type of language which the students themselves need to read and write. Thirdly, the reading material can provide the basis for reading comprehension exercises which focus on the way the text is structured and organised. An understanding of such organisation is a prerequisite for constructing a piece of coherent material. Thus, the comprehension exercise can provide a valuable basis for subsequent written production of a parallel text.

The language-learner should be asked to write only those structures and vocabulary items which he has practised orally and read in word recognition exercises. Thus he is already familiar with the words and structures and he is able to devote his whole attention to writing them. Writing should be started just after word recognition exercises. There are two main advantages of doing so:

(a) Writing reinforces oral and reading work. The language items already learnt become firmly fixed in the minds of pupils.

(b) Writing provides a change of activity and this helps in reducing monotony.

Mechanics of Writing

(i) To make letters of the right shape and size.

(ii) To have proper spacing between letters, words and lines.

(iii) To use capital letters and punctuation marks correctly.

(iv) To have a fluent hand movement in writing.

Writing: Penmanship

Writing is not an easy thing for a small pupil to learn because it requires a very fine control of the small muscles of the fingers and the wrist.

A child has a great difficulty in controlling even his larger muscles, e.g., watch him trying to throw a stone at an object. Training in penmanship should therefore proceed by easy steps:

(a) Fairly large movements using the finger in a tray of sand or chalk on brown paper: lines of various lengths and directions.

(b) Script writing: Small letters but larger size, arranged in groups, similar in shape.

(c) Spacing of letters is important for the neat appearance of the writing.

(d) The positions of body, arm, head and paper for writing be carefully watched by the teacher — body upright and parallel to desk, pencil to be held lightly.

The ability to write English cannot be acquired without adequate and regular practice. There will be two types of written work done by the students: (a) which is intended to conform a point already been taught and learnt by the students and (b) that where students are likely to make mistakes. The second category of written work must be carefully and regularly corrected by the language teacher. Teacher must ensure that corrections have been made and proper usage learnt through further practice.

Dictation

The objectives are:

(1) It is a method of fixing the spellings of words and the use of punctuation marks that have already been learnt.

(2) It provides good exercise in listening.

(3) It helps in teaching pronunciation.

(4) It helps in writing neatly and legibly at a reasonable speed.

If we accept these objectives, then two important corollaries follow:

(a) The passage to be dictated must be from the textbook which has already been studied.

(b) Since one of the purposes of dictation is to train students in listening, the sentences and phrases of the passage should not be repeated too often as it makes the students careless.

The passage for dictation should be read once before the students start writing, then it should be dictated in suitable units while they write and it should be read once again so that students can make necessary corrections. While dictating no sentence or phrase should be repeated. The students should be trained to listen to the whole phrase or sentence first and then write it. This practice will serve the purpose of inculcating the habit of careful listening.

Dictation should never be given solely as a test in early stages. Once again, it is a means of fixing what is already known, not a puzzle in which the teacher tries to defeat the pupil.

Dictation which results in mistakes is dangerous. It does no good at all; it does a great deal of harm. A safe rule to follow throughout the language course is never to give a dictation exercise in which there are words which the pupil has not seen before. After the first two years, a dictation exercise is useful for testing and for refreshing the pupil's memory as well as for reinforcing what he has learnt by oral practice and reading work.

Dictation, when given within the limits, is a valuable exercise because:

(a) It uses the hand as well as the eye for practising the shapes of words and this is far better than oral spelling by the name of letters.

(b) It fixes in pupil's mind the divisions of each sentence pattern because the good language teacher dictates division by division My daughter Rita/didn't go away/until yesterday. These divisions are brought to the pupil's notice by sound, by appearance and by muscular memory.

(c) Dictation uses the minds' eye — with which we photograph the spelling of a word. Spelling is largely a matter of visual memory, which writing helps.

Although in English the spelling does not always correspond with the sound, there are many groups of sounds which have a corresponding spelling. In the fixing of these, dictation trains the ear to listen carefully to the spoken sounds.

Dictation is one of the few exercises consistently employed throughout the history of language teaching. Until the end of the middle ages, it was the teacher's only resource to ensure retention. It is a means of fixing what is already known. Dictation trains the ear to listen carefully to the spoken English sounds.

Dictation seems to have been one of the key resources of the Direct Method. Teacher, for instance, faced with the problem of teaching his pupils how to distinguish the sounds of the new language, replaced those composition with dictation and was delighted with the results. Other Direct Method pioneers added a refinement to the exercise by stating: 'dictation is very stimulating to the pupils and serves as a useful test of their acoustic powers.' Besides, spelling was considered a legitimate aim of the dictation exercise.

12 TEACHING OF COMPOSITION

'Composition' is defined here to include both oral and written attempts to convey information, opinions, or emotions. It covers both factual and imaginative presentations. It includes the mechanics of paragraphing, punctuating and capitalizing, and it considers morphology, syntax, and semantics to the extent that they affect communication. It also considers the human content of composition — the personal expressions of voice, point of view, thought, creativity, and style.

Helping students to find something to say often begins with providing experiences that will stimulate authentic feelings, thoughts, and specially beliefs, which they will want to speak and write about. Films, pictures, posters, guest speakers, incidents acted out by students, discussions of literature, provocative articles and editorials from magazines and newspapers, etc., can provide experiences for generating ideas. The teacher's individual help is extremely important, and so are pupil's participation in classroom activities and discussions.

Within the framework of the good composition, the sentences march or trip toward an inevitable conclusion. The teacher's task is to help the student to see that each sentence can make its contribution to an entire paragraph, and each paragraph can make its contribution to a larger unit. Each word, phrase, each figure of speech, serves purpose. Correctness of spelling, punctuation, verb forms, and the like is taught because incorrectness detracts from receiving of the message. The message is of major importance, and nothing must be allowed to prevent its reception. Sentence structure is taught because not all possible forms of sentences are equally good for all purposes. Style is taught because some structures and some words are appropriate for certain purposes. But students do not learn writing best by hearing about it or reading about it; they must write, and they must talk about what they are going to write about. The task of teaching structure and style cannot be accomplished well by talking about it, nor with assigned readings, nor with making corrections. The teacher must ask questions, listen to what they have to say, respond, and should offer suggestions that focus on their writing compositions.

Composition literally means 'putting together.' English composition is concerned with two skills: (a) putting together words and phrases to make good English and (b) putting together one's thoughts so that when they are written they can be easily understood by the reader. It is obviously the important skill and a difficult one. The language-learner needs help in both aspects.

Composition is the art of putting thoughts into words. It is the ultimate aim of education and therefore, perhaps, the most important. aspect of English teaching and learning in schools.

There are two types of composition – Oral and Written. However, in our schools, composition is attempted in the form of written composition. Written composition should be preceded by plenty of oral work. One of the principal aims of teaching English is acquiring proficiency in speech. It is only when a student acquires a certain command of the language in speech that he is able to put down something worthwhile on paper.

Aim of Oral Composition

To develop the ability:

(a) To speak a few sentences correctly and continuously on a given topic,

(b) To describe any given topic,

(c) To discuss and debate,

(d) To arrange the ideas and express them clearly.

Mr. Robert Finch observes that good composition must grow out of a person's own experience. Children cannot write good composition unless they have something to say and only when they are interested. Earliest oral composition can be based on the children's personal experiences like

(a) Describing a picture,

(b) Describing a person, place or incident,

(c) Speaking a few sentences on a known subject,

(d) Discussing a topic of interest,

(e) Listening to a story and retelling it,

(f) Answering oral questions from a passage already read.

During this stage, the teacher should describe, narrate and introduce new words, phrases and sentences side by side. The child listens, observes, drills and assimilates the thoughts and ideas. The topic chosen for oral composition should be within the range of child's day to day experience. It should be kept in mind that the material of the language lesson is not language, but life itself. The language is the instrument we use to deal with the material: the slices of experience.

Good writing follows from correct speaking. Good writing can be based on fluent, correct speaking because a correct speaker depends on his ability to improve correct sentences, without reflection, out of the store of patterns which he has collected in his mind in prolonged and attentive listening.

Aim of Written Composition

To develop the ability:

(a) To write correct sentences on a certain topic,

(b) To write a paragraph correctly,

(c) To reply to letters,

(d) To convey written messages,

(e) To write stories,

(f) To write essays on given topics.

Pupil's first attempt at composition writing must be oral. Teacher should insist on correct oral English before they write. The pupils should be made to think out what they have to say and then be made to say in careful, deliberate speech with each word, article and preposition, distinctly pronounced. Whenever the teacher finds that written composition is not satisfactory, he should resort to oral composition as a corrective; remembering the principle that one who speaks well, will write well.

Controlled Composition and Free Composition

In Controlled Composition, students are given a certain framework within which they must limit their written work. In the first three years of language learning, it is advisable to limit the learners to controlled composition to make them avoid a number of mistakes. Early controlled composition can be in the form of transcription, answers to given questions from the Reader, Substitution Tables, rearrangement of sentences, joining and completion of sentences as well as transformation of sentences based on oral work.

Free Composition does not impose any restraint on the learners and they are left free to give full expression of their thoughts and ideas. Free composition is removing the props and leading students to unfettered writing.

Free Composition can start from the fourth year of learning English. The importance of oral work must be emphasized. Care should be taken to select the topics for free composition. They should be relevant to the students' world, arouse their interest and motivate them to think and express. No attempt should be made to kill the initiative. It will be worth experiencing enough variety in composition writing. The students may follow the usual pattern of Composition writing: Introduction — body — conclusion. But there should be no insistence on following this set pattern. It should be impressed upon the students the need to revise what has been written. The students should be trained to go through their written material and observe carefully the details like punctuation, spelling, use of articles, agreement between subject and verb, etc.

Guided Composition

When a child learns to walk, his first walking steps are guided. Similarly with English Composition, for pupils learning English as a foreign language, their first steps must be guided.

Procedure for Guided Composition

In a guided composition teacher guides every sentence to be written. He leads the pupils in their efforts. There is a lot of oral preparation of the pupils before they write.

Teacher takes a topic and writes it on the blackboard. Then he asks suitable questions to the pupils. He writes these questions on the blackboard. He writes the guide words by the side of the question. As he proceeds he impresses the need to follow punctuation rules and unconsciously creates a sense of the English sentence. After enough of oral preparation the pupils write the composition. While they are writing, teacher should provide additional guidance to them. Care should be taken to repeat the structural items and content words learnt earlier and the topic of composition should relate itself to personal experiences of the pupils.

Let us take an example. The first usual topic is 'My School.' The blackboard writing would appear as follows:

(a) What is the name of your school?

The name of my school is ____________

(b) Where is your school?

It _____ in ________ (town).

(c) How many classes has it?

It has _________ classes.

(d) How many teachers are there in your school?

There are __________________

The above example shows that guided compositions need a good preparation and a good preparation paves the way for good written composition.

Principles of Teaching Composition

Listening, speaking, reading and writing are the fourfold skills in language learning. 'Controlled composition' is the useful approach at the beginner's level. The students should not be given opportunities for making mistakes. Controlled composition writing infuses confidence and initiates students to continue writing step by step.

Composition in the early stages must be very carefully controlled. In a six years' course, free composition should not appear during the first three years. Looking at the age and intellectual development of pupils we may have it in the fourth year.

Mr. Robert Finch observes, good composition must grow out of one's personal experience. We write most powerfully when we feel most deeply, we write convincingly only when we have more to say.

The first kind of writing exercise to be given in the first year is copying or transcription. The object of this exercise is to allow pupil's mind to play around what has been taught in listening and speaking and thus fix it firmly. The pupil, during the first two years, should not be asked to write anything that he does not already know thoroughly through speech and reading. Every new structure should be practised by transcription after it has been thoroughly learnt.

The second kind of written exercise for the early stage is the writing of answers to given questions. The question helps the pupil with the words and the pattern required for the answer. Other types of written exercises for the beginners include substitution tables, exercises, rearrangements, sentence completion, matching, joining sentences with 'and', 'but', 'or' and simple description based on oral work. Transformation of sentences, e.g., questions into statements, affirmative statements into negative, present into past or future, singular into plural, etc., should also form a part of written composition.

Dictation is an important kind of writing exercise for the early stages. It is a means of fixing what is already known. It trains the ear to listen carefully to the spoken English sounds.

Reproduction exercises require ample oral preparation. They should, as far as possible, be based on the Reader. Guiding questions covering all the points must be written on the blackboard, while the pupils write their composition.

Free composition has no place at the initial stage of learning English. The students should not be given opportunities for making mistakes. This is the general pedagogic principle of teaching composition. Free composition may be given in the fourth year of the 6 year English course. In order to make them avoid mistakes, the pupil must be helped with ideas through oral preparation for the composition. He must also be helped to choose the right sentence patterns in which he can express those ideas. This can be done through oral preparation.

Pupil's first effort to composition writing must be oral. The pupils should be made to think out what they have to say it in careful, deliberate speech with each word, article and preposition distinctly pronounced.

All kinds of composition in the higher forms — paragraph, essay, precis, letter, paraphrase, translation — should be taught inductively to begin with. Specimens or models should be exhibited on the blackboard. They should be studied and discussed and the qualities of a good paragraph, essay, letter, etc., should be elicited from the pupils. They should then practise what they have learnt under the guidance of the teacher. Here also much of the work should be oral, followed by written work.

In teaching essay writing, the first stage should be the construction of the paragraph and the objective of the teacher should be to teach the principles of paragraph structure and to make the pupils practice in the formation of sentences that go to make up the paragraph. Paragraph contains one idea and should contain examples, details, comparisons, etc., to stress the idea.

In higher classes, more attention should be paid to continuous oral composition. This is the best preparation for continuous written composition. At the end of each stage in a composition discussion, pupil should be made to give orally in continuous sentences what has been discussed. Whenever the teacher finds that written composition is not satisfactory, he should resort to oral composition as a corrective, remembering the principle that one who speaks well will write well.

The main purpose of teaching composition is to enable the pupil to express himself clearly and accurately, to see things for himself and to describe them. Composition writing should train his imagination, develop his powers of thinking and reasoning, so that eventually he develops a feeling for the language, a love for and appreciation of good literature.

Correction of Written Composition

Correction must aim at developing creative impulse in the learner and must be appreciated. When certain mistakes are pointed out, teacher must make it a point to bring to the learner's notice that mistakes spoil good work. So the approach of the teacher must be both positive and negative and not negative alone.

The purpose of correcting composition is fourfold:

(a) To discover and correct mistakes,

(b) To check whether the pupils are able to arrange their ideas and express them clearly,

(c) To judge whether the matter is properly presented in written form,

(d) To inform pupil as to how he is compared with the standard expected of him.

A well-devised plan of correction is necessary. Teacher must not correct too many errors at a time. In the early stages, teacher should concentrate on spelling, punctuation, use of capitals, legible writing and so on and not about minor errors as the incorrect use of adjectives or metaphors. In the later stage he should attach more importance to fluency, clarity of expression and construction of sentences rather than to correct spelling. As Mr. Hartog puts it, 'He should criticize not the bricks but the architecture.'

Large-scale marking in red and blue will only discourage pupils. Teacher should rather underline the mistakes and allow the pupil to correct himself. If he cannot do this, correction should take the form of more drill work to fill the gap of knowledge that may have occurred.

Teacher can make a list of common mistakes of the pupils from their composition work and discuss them in the class to remove any misunderstanding or doubt.

Teacher also reads the written essays in the class. The class is invited to participate in the discussion. But the ultimate judge of the success and failure is the writer himself, based upon the view of the teacher and his friends. A discussion of three or four essays on these lines generally covers the merits and demerits of the essays of nearly the whole class.

Mr. Ballard claims that this method develops the creative and the critical faculties of the pupils. Pupils are encouraged to find merits as well as demerits.

Moreover, when corrected work is returned, mistakes as well as teacher's remarks must be discussed. This discussion helps to drive home the points the teacher wishes to make. In this manner the correction work can be a means of teaching as well as testing.

Teacher must bear in mind the following points while correcting composition:

(a) Corrections should never discourage the pupil.

(b) Correction should make him pay attention to all the mistakes and give drills for practice.

(c) Teacher should show the pupil that he has read his composition work with interest and should criticize his work constructively, appreciating his good points.

(d) Corrections should be stepping stone to the improvement of pupil's composition work.

Teacher can draw pupil's attention to the mistakes by using certain symbols, the meanings of which should be known to them. These symbols should be easy to understand, clear to read and be self-explanatory. Some symbols are as follows:

SP – Spelling error

A – Article

P – Punctuation

E – Bad English

Pupils should be taught to revise their work carefully before giving it to the teacher for correction.

Correcting Errors in Written Composition

There appears to be five distinct techniques of dealing with errors in written composition: (a) the teacher corrects the script; (b) the teacher deals with errors through marginal comments and footnotes; (c) the teacher explains orally to individual students; (d) the teacher uses the error as an illustration for a class explanation; (e) the teacher gives sufficient clues to enable self-correction to be made by students. All these techniques have their significant roles in correction and the teacher, after considering the nature of the errors, their frequency, and the standards of the class as well as that of the student who made the error, must decide which technique is likely to be most effective. The experienced teachers would agree that self-correction is the most effective way of extinguishing composition errors, but unless the clues given are quite clear and are interpreted correctly, worst confusion is likely to arise. It would appear then that there is no single standard method of dealing with composition errors, and it is the teacher, who must make a choice between the most appropriate and effective of several techniques used in correcting composition errors.

Teaching of Spelling

Spellings constitute the problem area for English language learners. English spellings are erratic as English is not a phonetic language.

Spellings in English are most irregular and illogical. The famous linguist Max Muller once said, 'English spelling is a national misfortune to England and an international misfortune to the rest of the world.'

Irregularities of English Spellings

(a) Same sound but different spellings: rite, write, right, etc.

(b) Similar spellings but different sounds: but, put, come home, great, cheat, etc.

(c) Words with silent letters: right, knight, doubt, palm, etc.

Causes of Poor Spelling

(i) English spelling does not correspond to pronunciation, e.g., to, two; seas, cease, seize; cut, put; come, home; bound, wound, etc.

(ii) New method of teaching reading (Look and Say Method) is the main cause for poor spelling where attention is given to the general shape or pattern of the word as a whole and not letters which constitute the word.

(iii) Pupils are not trained to observe words carefully — careful observation needs to be inculcated in the learners to instill right spellings.

(iv) Stress on oral work causes poor spellings — because necessity of spelling comes only in written work.

(v) Teachers do not employ suitable methods to teach spelling.

Method of Teaching Spelling

The aim of all spelling instruction should be to make the spelling of familiar words more or less automatic. The pupils should develop a spelling sense so that a faulty spelling looks wrong.

(i) Incidental Method: Teachers must draw the pupils' attention to the spellings of words as and when they occur in prose and composition lesson.

(ii) Drill Method: Teacher may group words according to sounds, meanings and their spellings. In this way, four lines of approach are coordinated, i.e., visual, oral, auditory and motor.

(iii) Look, Say and Write: Teacher writes the word on blackboard, utters the word along with the spelling. Then the pupils speak the word along with spellings and copy down in their notebooks.

(iv) Letters Written in Flashcards: The letters are mixed together. The pupils are asked to frame words using the various letters written on the flashcards, presented before them.

(v) Gramophone Records: There are gramophone records available on which the words along with the spellings are spoken. The record is played and the pupils listen to the records.

(vi) Interesting Games for Teaching Spelling: A few words are written on Blackboard. Pupils look at them for sometime. Then they are asked to speak those words along with their spellings by keeping their back towards Blackboard.

The blackboard should be the constant companion of the teacher of spelling. When the spelling of a new word is to be taught, it should be written on blackboard. Teacher should never exhibit wrong forms of spelling on blackboard, while presenting the words on blackboard for the purpose of teaching spelling; only a few words should be presented at a time.

The English teacher should be innovative enough to make the teaching of spelling interesting and effective.

Remedial Programme for Improving Spelling

Spelling is a sensory motor habit acquired by motor responses to certain sensory stimuli. The sensory stimulus is generally a written or printed word in reading. The eyes must be trained to see the word as a whole and in its component elements. The ears must be trained to hear the component sounds one by one, to catch the word as a whole and the order of sounds in uttering the letters and syllables. With these visual and auditory images the muscles of the hand and the fingers must form definite and ready association of movements.

The spelling involves sight, hearing, the muscular movements of the arm, the hand and the fingers — all these must be perfectly harmonized and coordinated before the spelling of a word can be mastered.

Words to be correctly spelt must be presented very vividly. Pronunciation of the word should be loud, clear and emphatic. Blackboard writing should be bold and transcription should be very legible.

The meaning of the word should be thoroughly explained before the pupil learns to spell it. Such an explanation make associations in his mind richer and more concrete. The words, instead of being arbitrary jumbles of letters become living, meaningful tools needed in written expression.

New words should not be introduced in an off-hand manner. Teacher must arouse the interest of the pupil in the new word and relate it to words already under reference.

In correcting pupils' written work, teacher should not merely mark errors in spelling but write out the correct order of letters on Blackboard.

For correct spelling pupil should be able to recognize words as a whole. A very important method is the presentation of words in groups formed on some intelligible plan, e.g., Con/ver/sa/tion, etc.

In the early and later stages of teaching spelling, pupils should be given a good deal of help by asking:

(i) Put the letter 'd' in place of a letter and make a new word: work, mark, grew, going.

(ii) Put in the missing letter: Chil-ren, g-ass, b-ought.

Dictation is a device which helps pupils to be conscious of spelling peculiarities.

Spelling Bees: This is specially useful in finding out those learners who are weak in spelling. By making a note of pupils' errors in spelling, the teacher can prepare a useful list of words for revision and re-teaching, if necessary. The words to be used in the contest can be selected from the class Reader or from a specially prepared spelling list. Two teams, composed of 10 to 12 pupils sit facing the class. At a given signal from the 'question master,' who can be the teacher, the first pupil gives a word to his opponent and asks him to spell it. A second attempt may be allowed; one mark is scored for every correct answer. A team may, however, refrain from asking the same question twice. To add interest to the contest, the teacher can signal correct answer by ringing a bell or a similar device.

HPH

13 INSTRUCTIONAL DEVICES AND ACTIVITIES FOR TEACHING ENGLISH

The words alone may not suffice to carry the pupils over into the imaginary situations for which the words are intended to build. Moreover, in order to make the entire teaching-learning process of English language learning lively, interesting and comprehensible, the teachers need to take the help of various devices in the classroom teaching-learning process.

(1) The Blackboard: It has great possibilities for pictorial representation; for writing the lists of new words or paradigms on it. The value of quick sketches on blackboard by the teacher for giving meaning or situation and thereby helping the pupils to picture what they are hearing about, is worth mentioning.

Technique of blackboard drawing: The blackboard drawing is a rapid sketch, not necessarily accurate. The essentials are indicated only and no unessential details are shown. The great advantage of blackboard drawing is that it takes shape under the eyes of the pupils. The blackboard drawing, built up like a living organism in front of the class, has a special life of its own, drawn with a running commentary from the teacher. It is, in itself, a means of relating language to experience. A figure may be rubbed out and rapidly redrawn in a new position to give the illusion of movement.

(2) Pictures: Either made by the teacher or brought for classroom teaching can be divided into two categories: (a) those designed primarily for classroom teaching and (b) those used primarily for decorating the classroom and giving a background that conveys a visual impression of the country where the language is spoken. Both are important, but they have different uses and should be handled differently.

Uses of pictures for practising the tenses: One way to get plenty of practise of the tenses is to ask about what the people in the picture are doing, have done, will do, and will have done in two hours' time.

Pictures printed in a textbook: If well drawn and brightly coloured, can contribute enormously to the attraction for the textbook and set each lesson in its appropriate visual setting.

Projected pictures: These are of two types:

(a) Filmstrips or slides and (b) Motion Picture films.

The film strip is the handiest medium for projection. The great advantage of the filmstrip is the possibility to stop at a picture as long as one likes — to search for clues, reflect and comment on it, discuss it, ask what it is leading on to, and recall what came before it, and then back to an earlier picture to see if one had remembered accurately. The filmstrip can be used for past, present and future.

The motion picture films have an added advantage. They can catch greater attention of pupils. There are different types of moving films like animated drawings, films with actions and dialogues or films with commentary only. The great disadvantage of the moving film for ordinary teaching is that it gives no time for reflection. The audience has to submit to the influence of the film and accept what it gives until the film is over. The moving film can hardly be used for an informal commentary by the teacher and a discussion as it goes along unless the sound is cut out. Even then the movement is too rapid for effective discussion to be possible.

In the natural process of learning a language we have natural speech-forms emerge from action, the less reflection is there on the language. Reflection allows comparison with the mother tongue and this produces difficulty. Normal photographic film might be better as there is a greater degree of authenticity and richer possibility for situation and action to hold the attention while language falls into its natural place in the background.

Adapting Moving Films to Classroom Use: For classroom teaching purposes, the film can be played silent with the sound switched off and given a simplified commentary within the vocabulary range of the pupils.

(3) Flashcards: For flashing in the classroom, useful for teaching reading, teaching vocabulary.

(4) Charts: Printed charts used for presenting language items.

(5) Tape-recorder: An audio aid used for (a) teaching pronunciation, (b) model reading or reading aloud, (c) conversations, discussions, (d) school broadcasts, which can be recorded and then played back for the class at the convenient timings, (e) reading verses and poems, etc.

(6) Television: It provides an opportunity to a large number of pupils to learn from a single experienced teacher. A good television teacher provides model of correct speech not only to the pupils but also to the less gifted classroom teacher.

Broadly speaking, language teaching consists of presentation, practice and production. Television can handle the first stage, i.e., presentation very well, quite often better than the classroom teacher because it has access to a wide variety of audio-visual aids. But television is not as well suited for the second stage, i.e., practice drill, due to lack of feedback from the pupils. The third stage, i.e., production is the least suitable on television because the medium is unidirectional. However, television gives extended practice in listening to language used in realistic social situations. After the television lesson, the classroom teacher must do the follow up in his classroom teaching by carrying on where the television teacher left off.

Television lessons can be syllabus-based or enrichment programmes. Purely enrichment programmes is not possible with our limited resources. Nor would they be desirable at the very early stages of language learning. As the essential prerequisite to enrichment programme, television programmers would have to be syllabus-based with an element of enrichment.

Television can never replace the classroom teacher who has advantage of being in direct communication with the class.

(7) Video Tape is a major format for motion picture viewing, which has grown steadily as a medium for showing motion pictures in educational setting. Video tape is less expensive than film. Many centers of education and training have established video libraries for educational purpose.

(8) The Radio occupies a very significant place in the teaching of English. It provides good learning experiences as it provides listening practice and oral work. The radio lessons should be well organised in the classrooms. The classroom teacher should make a proper introduction, keep the necessary visuals like picture, charts and maps ready for display and use when required. After the radio lesson is over, there should be oral and written reinforcement on the points of the lesson being broadcast.

(9) Language Laboratory: It has introduced automation in the classroom teaching. As AS.Hayes puts it, 'A language laboratory is a classroom or other area containing electronic and mechanical equipment, designed and arranged to make foreign language learning more effective than is usually possible without it.' Robert Lado defines it as 'a special room where students may practice speaking and listening with the aid of tape recorders, earphones, microphones and/or other sound equipment chiefly as an audio-lingual-supplement to class-work.' The purposes are: (a) Listening — to develop the ability to understand the language spoken at normal speed, (b) Imitation — to pronounce the sounds with stress, rhythm and intonation, (c) Repetition — to practice the spoken English, (d) Semantic drill — to practice in putting words in suitable contexts, (e) Practice in reading and (f) Testing.

It was in 1947, that the Louisiana State University in U.S.A set up a rudimentary type of language laboratory, whose creation was the result of experiment in language teaching made during Second World War. In U.K., the first language laboratory came into operation as late as in year 1961. In India the language laboratory made its appearance sometime in the mid-sixties. However, even today the language laboratory facilities are not easily available.

Language laboratories are of five types ranging from the simplest to the most complex. They are as follows:

(i) Audio Passive (AP): In this type of language laboratory, the student is provided with a headset with the help of which he is able to listen to the teacher speaking into the microphone or listen to the tape-recorder or the gramophone. The student can receive the lesson and reproduce it. However, his oral responses cannot be checked by the teacher unless he is standing by the student's booth. This is the simplest and the most inexpensive type of language laboratory. It helps concentration on materials received through the headset as the headset keeps off extraneous noise, thus helping concentration. The disadvantage is that the students' responses cannot be checked by the teacher.

(ii) Audio Active (AA): In this type of laboratory the student can listen to the lesson and repeat the same into the microphone which is inset in the microphone itself. This type of language laboratory has a certain advantage over the AP type as the student can listen to his own voice and compare it with that of the teacher.

(iii) Audio Active Comparative (AAC): In this type of language laboratory, the student can listen to his lesson, repeat it in the microphone and record his own response on the tape provided in the booth. He can play back the tape at a later stage and compare his response with that of his teacher and effect improvement.

(iv) Audio Active Comparative with Control (AACC): In this type of laboratory, the students' response can be controlled by the teacher from the console. The teacher can monitor the student individually and correct him without disturbing others.

The AACC Language laboratory is the most useful since it makes it possible to teach student at his own pace. When the teacher wants to address the entire group of students he can do so by stopping all the students' recorders.

The AACC language laboratory is costly and complex in its mechanism. Its operation and maintenance require the services of a technician. For its effective functioning, the air-conditioned room is generally desirable.

Mere installation of a language laboratory is not guarantee that improvement in linguistic skills will occur automatically. Good outcome demands (a) equipment of good quality with potential for a variety of learning experiences, (b) teacheres skilled in handling equipments, (c) materials prepared specifically with regard to the goals of the language learning course and techniques of laboratory learning and (d) careful allotment of laboratory time.

(10) Three Dimensional Representation: Actual representation of an action dramatically represents the action better than any picture can, because with it, we have movement and the third dimension.

(11) Puppetry: A convenient extension of classroom drama is puppetry. Children who are too shy to speak fluently in front of a class can often speak quite fluently if they are behind a screen and speaking for a. puppet they are manipulating with their hands. The making of puppets is a simple and fascinating activity that can be directed and carried out through the language being learnt; the activity helping fix the language-pattern and incidental explanations in the mind. Puppets, once started in the beginners' class can be continued right up through the higher level of the school with growing degrees of elaboration in the making and display of the puppets and growing degrees of sophistication in decor, production and in the nature of the plays produced.

(12) The Sand-table: A small heap of sand on the floor of the teacher's platform or in the corner of a room can be quite an effective aid for language-learning. One of the advantages of the sand-table is that it is transitory. It is an approximation, a hint, sufficient to set the imagination working. Thereafter, the imagination may be expected to take over the duty of keeping the scene in the mind's eye. A sand-table does not take the place of imagination, it stimulates the students to find expression in words.

Miscellaneous Visual Aids

Every language classroom should have a calendar to make pupils talking about the date easy. There should also be an old clock with hands that can easily be moved, or simply a clock-face for learning to tell the time. The clock-face can be made out of cardboard; the clock-face makes easy to teach and practise the use of the past and future tense. A mirror on the wall is valuable aid in teaching pronunciation. Also a small pocket mirror of each member of the class helps observe the shape of the mouth as he pronounces sounds that give him difficulty.

Once the pupil has got used to what the correct shape feels like and has learnt to bring his lips automatically to that shape when he utters the sound, he has overcome his difficulty in pronouncing the sounds correctly.

The Classroom Window: Link with the Real World: Although what one sees from the classroom window is not within the control of the classroom teacher yet it can be considered as an useful visual aid. The window presents a sample of the life of the world outside the school — the only accessible link with everyday life! Roads, houses, traffic, a railway station, factory, trees and garden and actions going on there. The language teacher may welcome the opportunities it gives for natural and effective use of language related to easily perceived samples of living. The classroom language teacher may sometimes spend ten or twenty minutes at the window, talking about what can be seen outside the window and afterwards make a rough representation of the principal features on the blackboard for further discussion.

Learning a language is a part of growth; like growth it can be assisted and stimulated; it cannot be forced or hurried. Teacher must set and exact a high standard of diligence and application and his reward will lie in enabling a number of individuals to be more efficient in their daily lives, more ready to communicate with their fellows, more aware of themselves and be more fully and articulate human beings.

DEVICES AND ACTIVITIES FOR LANGUAGE LEARNING

Language Games

Language Games occupy an important place in language learning, as they offer change, challenge, spirit of discovery and completion. When learning is combined with recreation, it becomes interesting. It is the play-way method, utilised for learning. It aims to encourage 'language learning without tears.'

Language games are useful for the informal learning of aural comprehension, oral expression, reading and writing. Because they involve active participation, games are suitable right from the beginning stage of learning.

(i) Oral Games: This is the game for beginners. The class is divided into two groups. The groups are asked to put several pictures in the box. A student from one group is asked to choose a picture. The student is asked to name it. Marks are given accordingly to both the groups and winning group is announced.

(ii) Reading Games: Read and do. Teacher writes a sentence. The class acts as per the sentence and say with actions. Teacher uses flashcards showing commands: Open the door, shut the window, stand up, etc. The student reads and acts.

(iii) Matching Games: Teacher shows the pictures and asks the student to select the card having the sentence appropriate to the picture.

(iv) Writing Games: (a) Crossword Puzzles — solving the puzzles with the right word. (b) Jumbled words and sentences — asking a student to write the correct sentence from the jumbled words displayed on blackboard, e.g., dog yesterday friend my bought a.

(v) Magician's Game: The student is asked to change one word into another by changing only one letter at a time. Each change must itself constitute a word.

e.g., change 'dog' into 'cat'

Dog cat

Dog dot cot cat

(vi) Spelling Games:

(a) Teacher writes a word on blackboard, preferably in capital, e.g., Teacher. Then he asks his students to write as many meaningful words as possible out of component letters. He then makes three columns, one for 3 letter words, next for four letter words, and third column for 5 letter words, e.g.,

Teacher

CAR	HEAR	TEACH
THE	HARE	THERE

As many as 45 words can be formed out of the word, Teacher. Teacher can create a sense of competition among students by asking every student in turn to contribute one word.

(b) Teacher divides the class into two groups. Teacher writes a word on blackboard and makes two columns, one for Group A and the other for Group B. Group A is asked to suggest a word that begins with the final alphabet of the words given by Group A.

Thus two groups continue to find words which begin with the final letter of each other's words.

(c) Another interesting game is to provide a contextual sentence in which one word is written in capital letters. Students are asked to rearrange the alphabets and make a meaningful sentence, e.g.,

(1) CHARM is the third month of the year.

(2) Sunil's house is made of NOTES.

(3) I use SHOE to water the plants.

Spelling games have a value. It infuses a healthy play spirit in the pupils. Class is stimulated to make an effort and concentrate on the learning of spellings, which is otherwise monotonous.

(vii) Games In Communicative Activities:

(a) 'Guess the Picture' game:

Teacher has a set of flashcards with picture. He selects one card and asks his students to guess what it is.

(b) 'What' and 'where' game:

Teacher displays a material and asks, 'What is it made of?' 'Where do we find it?' 'What is its use?'

(c) 'Information Gap' exercise:

Teacher skilfully combines the structures to let the students fill in the information gap.

An imaginative and resourceful teacher can devise several games which help language learners' learning the language with pleasure and interest and thereby developing the linguistic skills.

Story-telling, dramatisation are other useful devices.

Dramatisation

Dramatisation helps in language learning. Active participation, observation and cooperation help a great deal in learning a language. Dramatisation provides these essentials. Dramatisation gives life to the lesson. It serves as an excellent description in speech, poise and self confidence. It helps in the building of vocabulary. A school play is the most effective expression of the pupils' linguistic skills. Mr. F.G. French says, 'Dramatisation is a practical aid to learning which should be employed frequently in ordinary class time for teaching purposes. It has many valuable advantages. It does everything for the pupil which the reading book can do and it does many things which the reading book cannot do and does much better.' A story becomes vital and interesting by dramatisation. Acting catches the imagination of the pupils.

Dramatisation is a test of the comprehension of pupils. When they stage a story, they have full understanding of the story. Words and sentences used in the dramatised story are memorised by the pupil and become his own. They are retained in his memory for a long time.

Because of dramatisation, pupils get opportunities to work together for a common end. Class time does not provide opportunities for the teamwork. Dramatisation serves this purpose best. The shy pupil gets confidence while acting his role and find that he can speak aloud for all to hear without making a mistake.

Mr. F.G. French has suggested the following kinds for dramatisation:

(a) Dialogue between two persons: Doctor and patient, shopkeeper and customer, employer and an applicant for employment.

(b) Dramatisation of incidents seen in the street, in real life, such as a man paying a taxi driver.

(c) Little plays to track some simple rules of hygiene: health, safety on the roads, good manners, law and order, etc.

(d) Historical plays: history of the school, of the town, of the country, of the tribe or race; incidents from the lives of famous men.

(e) Stories — either from the textbook or from some other sources.

Teacher should select lesson for the purpose of dramatisation to suit the stage of pupils' learning.

Dramatisation encourages the learners to use the foreign language in a functional situation. It includes dramatic reading of short plays, acting memorized conversation, playing the role of a famous historical character. Learners may participate in various stage activities such as prompting, managing, directing under the teacher's supervision.

Dramatising a scene, a dialogue or a story always adds an interesting note to the routine of classroom teaching. Learners, specially younger ones, are usually eager to take part. Action in the foreign language encourages its oral use in a natural situation. The following suggestions may help in the use of dramatisation:

(a) Use dramatisation on the very first day of language instruction. Familiar greeting such as 'Good morning, this is Mr. ....' can be dramatised during the early lessons. Free conversation and role-playing can be practised by more advanced students.

(b) While part of the class is acting, the rest of the learners should be asked to observe and criticise. Some may be asked to comment on the action or on the way the ideas are expressed.

(c) While dramatising, expressive pronunciation, proper gestures and facial expression should be emphasized.

(d) While reading or explaining the proper tone of voice, physical movement should be used to emphasize important points.

English Club

English Club can be organised as a part of the language teaching scheme after the students have made progress in learning English.

The activities of such a club will help develop fluency in the use of the language.

How to Organise the Club?

(a) The teacher should give a brief talk on the organisation, working and usefulness of a model club in order to arouse the interest and enthusiasm of the students.

(b) A constitution is drawn up with the assistance of the class. The office-bearers are elected from among the students themselves.

(c) A programme of activities for the term or year should be drawn up by the committee of office-bearers. The programme should be simple and interesting, in keeping with the age, abilities and interests of the student members of the club. It can include items like language games, dramatisation, play-reading, prepared speeches, debates and panel discussions, book reviews, elocution contest, poetry recitation and song. The programme can also include film-shows, lectures by invitees, the exchange of correspondence with foreign or local clubs, social gatherings and visits to museums etc. An annual or a quarterly souvenir containing the programmes of work, pictures, etc., can also be undertaken by the club.

Use of the Library

Library reading is very helpful in developing linguistic skills. A valuable way of encouraging reading is to provide time in school for children to read what they like. A couple of periods a week taken in school library, gives the language teacher the chance to talk to children individually about their interest and their reading habits and thereby can direct the reading habits of the children.

There are some useful suggestions for training children to use library effectively in order to enrich their knowledge and vocabularies. For the language teacher, the running of class library is very useful. A class library can be run in the following ways:

(a) If the school authorities have sufficient funds, books can be purchased for the class library from this fund.

(b) Each pupil of the class may buy one book suggested by the English teacher and the book is registered for the class library along with the name of the author. These books can be distributed to the whole class in rotation. Children should be made to feel that books are there to be read. The English teacher should continuously invite their attention to the class library. Pupils should be asked to keep a notebook in which they should note down the name of the book, the author and a very brief summary of the subject matter. The subject matter should suit the age-level of the pupils for whom the books are to be used. Teacher may ask questions on the subject matter. He may have the stories told or prominent characters described. Small skits may be arranged, based on the books read.

The habit of reading books can be cultivated more easily in this manner than any other method. The pupil must read books in the class, out of the class, in the school, in the home and out of the school or home. The main idea of extensive reading in language-learning is to train pupils to read books from the library independently. Therefore a regular practice in the art of using reference books in the library should be given.

Use of Mass Media in Language Learning

The language teacher is constrained by the four walls of the classroom and can bring in the outside world only a limited way by means of make-believe.

Mass Media, i.e., television, radio, newspaper can help in widening the language experience of the pupils. The greatest merit of mass media is that it can create a far greater variety of situations than the classroom teacher. The pupils can be exposed to the language at a railway situation, at a bus stop, in various social situations.

Mass media (television, radio) provides an opportunity to a large number of pupils to learn from a single experienced teacher. A good television/radio teacher provides a model of correct speech not only to the pupils but also to the less gifted classroom teacher.

The attitude of the classroom teacher towards mass media is very important. The mass media is not going to replace the teacher but is working with him. The right attitude can be developed through teachers' seminars where the teacher is trained in the use of the medium. In any TV period, the classroom teacher plays a greater role than the television teacher.

The TV/Radio Programme is used as supplementary instruction and therefore there should be complete coordination between the transmitting and the receiving end.

In the teaching-learning process, three factors are very important: (1) curriculum, (2) learning experiences and (3) evaluation. For language learning, proper learning experiences should be provided to the children. It is the learning experience that effectively brings about the desired change in the child in accordance with the predetermined objective. In order to provide adequate and varied learning experiences to the language learners, mass media should be utilised to a great extent.

Communication by T.V. is effective because it can transmit a wide range of audio-visual material including still pictures, films, objects, specimens, etc. Television can bring models of excellence to the viewers, in the form of great poets, great dramatists, etc. It can bring the world of reality to the classroom either through a live broadcast or through film. The medium provides us sounds with sights and it overcomes the distance barriers. The teacher, however enthusiastic and competent he might be, has his own limitations. He cannot overcome the barriers of distance and time.

However, mass media has a great limitation. It is one-way communication device. Television/Radio moves ahead at a constant speed. There is no direct participation of the learners in educational television and radio programmes.

Correlation in English Language Teaching

The concept of correlating various subjects in the curriculum is fairly modern development in education which believes that all knowledge should be interrelated in such a manner that the pupils are able to see isolated facts as one comprehensive whole. Based on the Gestaltian principle of regarding things as a whole — the whole being more meaningful than the sum of its parts — the concept of correlation in teaching-learning process has gained great strength and importance.

English language has been divided into its different branches – prose, poetry, grammar and composition; not because each aspect is different from the other, but to enable the teacher to pay attention to these various aspects in greater detail.

Correlation between Grammar, Composition and Prose

Grammar and composition are essential parts of the whole English language course. Grammar should be mainly taught for the sake of composition and reading. It is not a subject in itself but a useful handmaid to Composition and Reading. Grammar is a means to correct faulty composition and faulty speech and helps in comprehension of reading and prose. Therefore all grammar teaching must be linked with prose and composition lessons.

Grammar book must be based on the Reader and should contain sufficient material to cover what the class has already done or is doing in oral and reading lessons. Both the Reader and the Grammar book should follow a definite plan, the later depending on the former. Grammar must go hand in hand with oral work and reading. A good Grammar book has to be graded to fit the vocabulary and the structures which the pupil has learnt in prose lessons.

In the first year of English language teaching, there should be no teaching of formal grammar but the pupils should be encouraged to have the grammatical exercises at the end of the prose lessons, which must be so graded to give knowledge of subject and predicate, agreement of the verb with the subject, the use of capitals at the beginning of the sentences etc.

Grammar must grow out of the prose lessons and the oral work in class. During oral work, pupil picks up new structures and he should be made to drill them in such a way that he can use it easily and readily. While doing each prose lesson teacher must consider the grammatical points to be dealt with and as the lessons proceed, the grammar work grows with them.

Grammar, rightly taught, must correlate speech, in which the sentence is a unitary whole. The learner displays his knowledge of Grammar in speaking grammatically correct sentences. This is called Functional Grammar and is more the concern of the teacher than the student as the student gains his knowledge unconsciously.

During reading lessons pupils absorb a large amount of vocabulary, structures and sentence-patterns. Grammar book is more a book of reference and must supplement the grammar exercises found at the end of each prose lesson in the Reader.

Composition is closely related with grammar and prose. Earliest composition writing is always based on prose lessons. Controlled composition takes the form of transcription and answers from prose lessons. Basically, composition is nothing but the use of grammatical structures with vocabulary that has been enriched by prose and poetry lessons.

• Every aspect of English language can be so linked with the other during teaching-learning process that all the elements of the language get cemented into a sound workable knowledge of the language.

As for external correlation with other subjects in the school curriculum, the teachers must ensure continuity through each of the main subjects, namely, science, mathematics and social studies. All the items of knowledge should be presented in an integrated form. They should be integrated with the actual life of the child, based on his needs and activities.

HPH

14 QUALITIES OF GOOD ENGLISH TEXTBOOK: ITS ANALYSIS AND EVALUATION

We must recognise that under the heading 'English' there is included a variety of skills to be taught and a vast amorphous mass of material to work with, but very few obvious facts to teach.

The material of English exists in the mind of the learner who is being taught. The English teacher aims to stimulate the learner to think and to clarify his own thoughts. He intends to stimulate the learner to feel and to become conscious of his feelings. The teacher cannot supply the thought; the teacher cannot supply the feelings. What the teacher can do and aims to do, is to put the learner into situations, real or imaginary, in which he will be compelled to think or to feel for himself in a particular way. In English we are not called to read a book only for the facts it contains; it can be read as an emotional experience in which the learner is encouraged to share. The aim of the English teacher must be to encourage the students to approach their reading with alert and critical minds and to develop a taste that will yield them greater profit and pleasure. That is no easy task for the English teacher. There is no direct road to success in dealing with this problem. Each English teacher will select his own material and work out his own approach.

We can teach without a textbook; we learnt out first language without the textbook, but to make the best use of time in the classroom and to avoid unintended repetition or the neglect of essential language patterns, the teacher is wise to have a textbook, at least in the background of his mind.

Each lesson in the textbook, should stand for a set of skills, a set of language patterns. Both teacher and pupil must realize that the language learning process does not begin and end in the textbook, but yet base their work on it.

The role of the textbook in a normal school language course may be summarized as follows:

(a) A guide for the teacher,

(b) A memory aid for the pupil,

(c) A permanent record or measure of what has been learnt,

(d) A means of extending linguistic experience beyond the local scene and the limited experience of the pupil,

(e) An exercise-ground for reading. A textbook is the central string round which the whole teaching-learning process is woven.

(f) It brings a system in the teaching work.

(g) Examples given in the books serve a very useful purpose.

(h) The textbook checks unnecessary repetition and omission.

The textbook is perhaps the most important of many visual aids in the teaching-learning process. In opening up the textbook, the teacher opens window to the world, which both show the world and let the light into the home.

The language teacher should evaluate the textbook so as to find out its good and bad points. Teacher must see the thematic content of the book:

A good language textbook must possess the following characteristics:

(a) Vocabulary used in the book should be well selected and properly graded. A good language textbook is written within a limited vocabulary. Vocabulary is introduced in the book based on the maxim: simple to complex. Whenever a new word is made to occur in a sentence or in a page, it is repeated in the subsequent pages so that learners may have full acquaintance with that word. All new words are clothed in structures with which the students are already familiar. The structures and new vocabularies used in a lesson should be written in the beginning of each chapter so that learners make effort to familiarise themselves with these language items.

(b) Structures must be placed in a scientific way. Whenever a new structure is introduced, it is to be clothed in the vocabulary already known to the students. In every lesson, the new structure should be printed in bold type to make students aware of the new structure introduced in the lesson.

(c) Subject matter contained in the book must be in keeping with the mental level of the students for whom the book is prescribed. Young students are familiar with home, family, school, toys, games, animals, festivals, etc. So the textbook for the beginners should have subject matter which deals with these activities. For the older students, there may be tales of actions, dramatics, fiction etc. depending upon their interests and needs.

(d) Social background of the learners is also to be kept in mind so that the students may have clear-cut understanding of the subject matter.

(e) The chapter in the textbook should be interrelated. Interlinks of the chapters would keep the students interested in the book. There should be variety in the different chapter contained in the book. The essays, stories, biographies of great men and poems should be mixed together so that the students find interests in reading the textbook.

(f) Illustrations in the textbook should be simple so that language practice by the learners should be possible through them. Pictures should be clear and to the point. For the younger students, there should be coloured pictures, appropriately placed. The activity pictures help the students to understand the activities described in the lesson. Teacher can explain several points by means of pictures without using the mother tongue. In the case of poetry lesson, several poetic ideas can be illustrated by means of pictures.

(g) Exercises at the end of each chapter should have practice material and testing material. The exercises should test as many language items as possible.

(h) Technical considerations are very important in case of every textbook. Good learning depends upon a good textbook. Its appearance, get-up, etc., should make the textbook attractive and pleasant to read. Following points in this respect are worth considering:

(i) Papers in the textbook should be of good quality. It should be soft and glossy so that the students may enjoy reading the book.

(ii) Printing should be neither too big nor too small. It should be free from error.

(iii) Binding of the book should be strong enough.

(iv) Size of the textbook should be neither too big nor too small, depending on the age-group of students for whom it is meant.

(v) Teachers' handbook should accompany a good textbook, which contains instructions regarding the use of the textbook and guidelines for teaching the various language-items contained in the lessons of the textbook.

The textbooks should be so designed and organised that a great deal of improvisation and adaptation by both the teacher and class is possible. No textbook can expect to appeal to all teachers or learners at a particular level. There are many ways of designing textbooks so that they can be used by a variety of learners with a variety of ultimate goals; they can be taught by a variety of teachers with a variety of teaching styles.

The teacher should not confuse his role with the role of textbook by identifying himself with the textbook. The textbook brings into the classroom what otherwise would remain outside.

HPH

15 ROLE AND RESPONSIBILITIES OF ENGLISH TEACHER

Multilingualism is a social reality in India. Oral and literacy skills in multiple languages are necessary for meaningful participation in the larger democratic, socio-political and economic system of the country. Starting with the mother tongue for family and community level communication, people need languages for regional communication, national level communication with wider context. Thus, promotion of multilingual competence is widely accepted as one of the goals of Indian Education.

With the advent of 21st Century, new perspectives and research on the status and role of English as the second language or most important foreign language in South-east Asia have been presented.

During the mid-1960s, a research team of nearly twenty specialists in English language teaching spent two and a half years studying the English teaching programmes of about two hundred schools in U.S. Two characteristics that finally emerged at the top of the list out of the research are: the intellectual climate of the school, and the quality of the English teachers. As far as English teachers were concerned, the first characteristic depended upon the second. Professional competence, dedication, enthusiasm and professional interest in the subject and in the students, apparently set the intellectual tone for students. The effective teacher is still the most significant factor in the English teaching programmes of the school.

English teachers need to be clear about their roles as teachers of language. As language teachers, they are not guardians of the language, protecting it from change. The English teacher can rather be a creative and stimulating teacher of a great language if he can successfully open the ears of this students to the many varieties of linguistic usage which constantly flow around us. If he can challenge his students to experiment with with many usage and styles and master them for his use, he would accomplish much. He should teach awareness, sensitivity, taste and discrimination, rather than rules: a few fixed and invariable forms. The use of English language should not be confined to a straight jacket of 'proper' forms, but enjoy the flexibility of expression and the vivid words and phrases that make the language dynamic and alive. Sound teaching of usage involves more than filtering out the impurities. Students must understand that the development of good language patterns depend on sensitivity to educated speech and the making of informed choices in usage.

Every teaching and learning act is an experiment. As with scientific experiments, teaching has its design, its form, its structure. Like the best experiments, it must be constantly willing to test untested assumptions. Every teaching act has its uncertainty, its risk. A teacher must accept the uncertainty of teaching and be willing to do little experimentation in the process with the knowledge of conditions favourable for that. It is a teacher who can create a classroom climate most favourable.

Related to the characteristics of adaptability, is the prerequisite to it – alertness. The successful teacher is physically, mentally, socially and politically alert. Being on the alert is being constantly alive, constantly aware of possibilities. It is constantly testing one's own potentials, as well as those of students, through constant experimentation in teaching and learning.

Teaching is a cognitive activity, and it is an imaginative activity. But it is also a moral activity and a social activity. The English teacher must be alert to all that this implies. An alert teacher is more likely to be an honest teacher and honesty is much needed in the classroom because it is much needed everywhere else in the real world. To be alert is to learn; and the more the teacher knows, the more inclined the teacher will be to encourage different points of view, related to learning.

The teacher, being truly human, is likely to have a sense of humour. Learning is apparently something like digestion. A person digests more readily if mealtime is enjoyable. A classroom is similar to a dinning room; the teacher is the host.

The capable English teacher is professional in outlook. That implies dedication to the profession of teaching English. Being professional calls for subscribing to professional magazines, attending professional meetings and seminars, getting involved with worthy professional activities. It includes following a carefully formulated code of professional ethics. In addition, an English teacher should be aware of changes in the teaching profession and of changes in the world at large. The teacher's knowledge should include language acquisition, analysis of discourse, resources for teaching, curriculum design, testing and research.

The teacher plays a central role in effective language teaching and learning and some of the most important developments in the language arts during the past decades have focused directly on the teacher. The image of teacher as professional carries with it a clear set of responsibilities for planning and decision making as well as a clear set of obligations in terms of knowledge and competence in structuring teaching and learning in the language classroom.

The curriculum is an important component of effective language learning. It represents a translation of teachers' goals and perception of students' needs into specific content and activities. Assumptions about the most effective approaches to curriculum and instruction have evolved rapidly. They provide teachers with the framework for issues of teaching and learning. These frameworks, in turn, shape the curriculum that students experience and the learning that results.

English teacher's task is to improve communication. Communication is divided into following parts:

COMMUNICATION

Sending ⟷ Thinking ⟷ Receiving

Speaking/Writing/Listening/Reading

This four-part division does not necessarily mean that each section will be equally emphasized in the classroom. Thinking, often called the fifth language art, bonds all four parts together as a meaningful process. Reading is broadly defined to include the reading and study of literature. Speaking and writing both involve study of the language (as do listening and reading), but because writing skills seem to take longer to develop than do speaking skills, teachers tend to devote more attention to the language of writing. Moreover, the daily functioning of the English language should be given attention. Students should have regular practice in using the language through a planned but flexible sequence of oral and written compositions.

Planning is the process of translating a teacher's vision and hopes into classroom realities. Whatever kind of classroom the teacher hopes to have, (open, informal or conventional and highly structured), planning will be necessary.

Good lesson planning is the art of mixing techniques, activities and materials in such a way that an ideal balance is created for the class. A classroom is almost always more complicated and unpredictable than most teachers care to admit, and teachers should be aware of this, as they plan. Planning will not eliminate the diversity and unpredictability of human learning; good planning takes such factors into account. The experienced, hard-working, creative teacher will be confronted with problems and situations, which he would deal with only by trial-and-error approaches. The more experienced and competent he becomes, the less likely he is to be surprised and devastated by the unexpected. Established teaching routines, however unimaginative or dull, can provide students with a certain sense of security; and sudden departures from these routines, particularly by a new and insecure teacher, may lead to confusion and hostility rather than learning.

The two overriding principles behind good lesson planning are variety and flexibility. Variety means involving students in a number of different types of activities and where possible, introducing students to a wide selection of materials. Variety makes learning for the students, interesting. Flexibility implies the teacher's ability to use different techniques in classroom teaching. Flexibility is also important when dealing with the plan in the classroom. The flexible teacher will be able to change the plan in demanding situations. Flexibility is the characteristic to be expected from the genuinely adaptable teacher.

Prior to consider planning for his classes, the teacher needs to know a considerable amount about three main areas: his profession; the institution, and the students. A well-prepared teacher needs to know a lot about his job before he can start to make successful plans. The teacher also needs to know a lot about the institution in so far as it is involved with his teaching. Finally, the teacher needs to know a considerable amount about his students. The teacher needs to know who the students are, what the students bring to the class and what the students need. Different types of students will need to be treated differently.

The role of the teacher will also depend, to a large extent, on the function he performs as controller, assessor, organiser, prompter, participant and resource person. The teacher plays the role of 'controller' when he is totally in charge of the class. The introduction of new language often involves the teacher in a controlling role, particularly at the reproduction stage. While conducting a drilling session, there is the perfect example of the teacher as controller. It is important to realise, however, that this control is not necessarily the most effective role for the teacher to adopt.

A major part of a teacher's job is to assess the students' work, to see how well they are performing or how well they performed. A difference has to be made, however, between correcting and organising feedback. Correction involves showing that incorrectness has occurred. Organising feedback is a major part of assessing students' performance so that they can see the extent of their success or failure. Here the teacher waits until an activity or task has been completed and then tells the students how well they did.

Two kinds of feedback can be distinguished: Content feedback and Form feedback. Content feedback concerns an assessment of how well the students performed the activity as an activity rather than as a language exercise. Content feedback centres on the content or subject matter of an activity: it aims to give students feedback on their degree of communicative efficiency. Form feedback, on the other hand, tells students how well they performed in terms of the accurate use of language. The teacher should take great care not to make form feedback dominant after communication activities: content feedback should usually come first and the teacher must decide when form feedback is appropriate and when it is not. It is vital for the teacher to be sensitive to his students in his role as 'assessor.' Perhaps the most important and difficult role the teacher plays is that of 'organiser.'

The success of teacher's activities depends on good organisation and on the students knowing exactly what they are to do. The main aim of the teacher when organising an activity, is to instruct exactly what the students task is, and then organise feedback when it is over. The organisation of an activity can be divided into three main parts. The first: the teacher gives a lead-in. This will take the form of an introduction to the teaching matter. When the lead-in stage has been accomplished, the teacher instructs. This is where he explains exactly what the students should do. Finally, the teacher initiates the activity. The 'lead-in-instruct-initiate-organise feedback' sequence can almost always be followed when the teacher is setting up activities in his role as 'organiser.' His job is to organise the activity as efficiently as possible.

Often the teacher needs to encourage students to participate in the activity or to make suggestions about how they may proceed in the activity. This is one of the teacher's important roles: the role of 'prompter.' The role of prompter has to be performed with discretion with the ideas that he should be helping his students only when necessary. Teacher as a 'participant' should participate in classroom activities to improve the classroom atmosphere; it will also give the students a chance to practice the language with someone who speaks it better than they do. Teacher as a 'resource' should always be ready to offer help when needed. The crucial responsibility of the teacher is to allow students to use the language as freely as possible, so that the classroom becomes a genuine language-learning community. This will require careful planning. Classroom teaching combines substance and technique. It requires a knowledge of content (substance) and the management of materials and procedures (techniques) in such a way that the best possible learning situation is created.

One of the most obvious features about the development of communicative ability is that it occurs through the processes inside the learner. The teacher can offer the kinds of stimulus to influence the course of development; the learner will attempt to follow a sequence of learning determined by his own natural processes. If one looks at foreign language learning as it occurs in the natural environment, it becomes clear that these processes can work without any teacher at all so long as the environment provides the necessary stimuli and experience. The concept of teacher as 'instructor' is thus inadequate to describe the overall function.

In a broad sense, he is a 'facilitator' of learning and may need to perform in a variety of specific roles, separately or simultaneously. These include the following:

(a) As general 'overseer' of his students' learning, he must aim to coordinate the activities so that they form a coherent progression, leading towards greater communicative ability.

(b) As 'classroom manager,' he is responsible for grouping activities into 'lessons' and for ensuring that these are satisfactorily organised at the practical level. This demands deciding on his own role within each activity.

(c) As language 'instructor', he will present new language items, exercise direct control over the learners' performance, evaluate and correct it, whenever necessary.

(d) As a keen 'observer,' he will let learning take place through independent activity, which will frequently be communicative activity. While such independent activity is in progress, he may act as 'consultant' or 'adviser,' helping where necessary. He may also move about the classroom in order to monitor the strengths and weaknesses of the learners, as a basis for planning future learning activities.

(e) As 'communicator' with the learners, he can stimulate and present new language items and participate in the situations without taking the main initiative for learning away from the learner themselves.

(f) As traditional 'dominator' of the classroom interaction, he is significant not only for methodological reasons, but also for his effect on human relationship within the classroom.

Besides, the English teacher needs to be interested in and sympathetic to his pupils. All this amounts to a demand for a cultured human being with a sympathetic personality, who has a clear grasp of the principles of his subject and who has an interest in his pupils trying to learn the language.

The teaching of an English teacher is consequently based on a direct contact with the feelings and thoughts of his pupils. He acts as stimulator, as a guide and as a refining agent for his pupils' thoughts and ideas, feelings and imagination. He must be able to inspire trust, so that pupils will readily express their thoughts and feelings without reservation, as children like adults, are shy of revealing themselves and will to do so to anyone who is distant or antipathetic. He must be able to teach children as a class and yet appreciate each one as an individual with unique emotions and thoughts. To a great extent these are the qualifications of all good teachers but there are necessary differences of attitude between the approach of the English teacher and that of others.

The National Council of Teachers of English (NCTE) published guidelines for the Preparation of Teachers of English Language Arts in 1986. In defining the roles of elementary and secondary teachers of English language, it recognized three categories: Knowledge, pedagogy and attitudes.

Knowledge:

(a) Teachers of English language need to possess growth in language maturity.

(b) Need to evaluate, select and use an array of instructional materials and equipment that can help students perform instructional tasks, as well as understand and respond to what they are studying.

Pedagogy:

(a) Teachers of English language must be able to select, design and organize objectives, stratifies and materials for teaching English language.

(b) Able to guide students in improving their processes of speaking, listening and writing abilities and reading for personal growth, information, understanding and enjoyment.

Attitudes: Teachers of English language must possess a commitment to continued professional growth in the teaching of English language. Personality, insight, knowledge, pedagogy and attitudes of teachers intertwine in each English language classroom.

English teachers need to be clear about their roles as teachers of language. As language teachers they are not guardians of the language protecting it from change. English teacher can rather be a creative and stimulating teacher of a great language.

In effective classrooms, the teacher's role needs to be one of collaboration, setting consistent high standards but postponing evaluation of the final product. Evaluation has an important role in most classrooms, but it is a role that needs to be separated from feedback on work in progress. Only in this way can the teacher offer support that allows tentative explorations of new learning. If evaluation intrudes too soon, students will retreat to the display of previous learning. They must know the proper methods and techniques for assessing students' language growth.

As English teachers they must understand the role of culture in language development and academic achievement: how students' cultural identifications affect language learning.

HPH

16 EPILOGUE

The spectacular advance of English language across the face of globe is a phenomenon without parallel in the history of languages. English is the principal language of the United States, Canada, Great Britain, Australia, New Zealand and of the newly independent countries such as the Bahamas, Jamaica, Barbados, Trinidad, Tobago and Guyana. It is the official language of more than a dozen African countries as well as of various British dependencies such as British Honduras, Gibraltar, Hong Kong and numerous islands in the Caribbean, and the Atlantic, Indian and Pacific Oceans. In India it has the title of 'associate official language' and is generally used in conversation between people from different parts of the country. In several other countries throughout the world, it is the unofficial second language.

In tracing the historical development of the English language, it is customary to divide it into three periods: Old English, which dates from earliest times to 1150; Middle English, 1150-1500; and Modern English, 1500 to the present.

The history of the English language may be said to have begun with the arrival in Britain of the Germanic tribes about the middle of the 5th Century. Angles, Saxons and Jutes crossed the North Sea from what is present day Denmark and the coast of north-west Germany. The inhabitants of Britain prior to this invasion spoke a Celtic language, which seems to have quickly given way to the new Germanic tongue. The Jutes, who came from Jutland, settled in Kent, the Isle of Wight, and along part of the Hampshire coast. The Saxons, who came from Holstein, settled in the rest of England, South of the Thames. The Angle who came from Schleswig, settled in the area extending northward from the Thames as far as Scotland, and it is from them that the word 'English' evolved. They came from the 'angle' or corner of land in present-day Schleswig-Holstein. In old English their name was 'Engle' and their language known as 'englise.' In the next several centuries four distinct dialects of English emerged. The Humber River divided the northern kingdom of Northumbrian, where Northumbrian was spoken, from the Kingdom of Mercia in central England, where Mercian was spoken. The West Saxon dialect developed in the Kingdom of Wessex, while Kentish was spoken in Kent. In the 7th and 8th Centuries Northumbria enjoyed political and cultural ascendancy in England, but in the 9th century both Northumbria and Mercia were utterly devastated by the invasions of the Vikings. Only Wessex preserved its independence and by the 10th Century the West Saxon dialect came to be the official language of the country. Since most surviving Old English works are then written in West Saxon, our knowledge of Old English is derived mainly from this dialect. (Katzner Kenneth, The Languages of the World, London and Henley, Routledge and Kegan Paul, 1975).

EFL, ESL and TESOL

The original term for teaching English to those who did not know it and for the area of expertise associated with it, was English as a foreign language, known for short as EFL. On the whole, this continues to be the British usage in referring to overseas teaching of English. The second usage of ESL refers to the learning of English in an English-speaking environment, such as by foreign students in England or in the United States. Finally, the third usage of ESL defines a second language as the official language of a nation which must be learnt by its citizens for full social, economic and political participation in the life of that nation. Australian Aborigines, British Gaelic speakers as well as immigrants learn English as a second language according to this definition. All three usages are common, but the third is to be preferred because it is the relationship between the super and subordinate groups within a nation which gives second language learning its significant characteristics and which distinguishes it from learning a foreign language, where attitudes are fairly neutral. In order to avoid the dichotomy, EFL and ESL became united in

TESOL, teaching English to speakers of other languages, which stands both for the field and for the international professional organisation, which was founded in 1966.

The Domain of TESOL

The teaching of English to speakers of other languages, as a professional field, is a relative newcomer to language teaching compared to the teaching of Greek and Latin. Similar to those languages, the spread of English has also reflected social conditions such as immigration, colonialism, military power, and trade as well as advanced scientific knowledge, and in the case of English, advanced technology.

The result has been a many-faceted picture of English teaching around the world. Basically, the field can be subdivided into four areas: EFL, ESL, bilingual education, and ESOD (English to speakers of other dialects) (Robinett, 1972).

EFL (English as a Foreign Language)

The study of English began primarily as learning English as a cultural acquisition, which would enable the learner to read the classics of Shakespeare and Milton. The purpose, objectives, and methods of this type of English study are similar to the study of French, German and Italian as foreign languages. Today, however, EFL overlaps with English as an LWC (Language of Wider Communication), as the major *'lingua franca'* of the world. Until the First World War, French had been the major language of wider communication within Europe, but after the Second World War this role has been taken over worldwide by English. This fact is reflected in the considerable investment in English teaching — in curriculum, textbooks, and teacher training, held by Third World countries where English language is seen practically as an instrumental means of international communication in a global system.

It is also reflected in the popularity of the adult English classes sponsored by the British Council around the world. The Regional English Language Centre (RELC) in Singapore can be cited as an example in this context. As far as language attitudes are concerned, the study of EFL is considered neutral. There are no external social, religious, or political pressures which enforce the study of English. It is rather a voluntary choice for instrumental or integrative purposes.

ESL (English as a Second Language)

The study of English language takes place in many parts of the world because English is an official language of that nation. This situation is almost always the result of colonization. Actually, the situations vary widely with countries which are commonly thought of as monolingually English, such as Australia and the United States, to countries which are notedly multilingual, such as Nigeria and India. The purposes and motivations for maintaining English as the official language vary as the situation's social, economic, religious and political factors vary. In India, English language is preferred by many as the national language to the alternative of Hindi. Along with the situations, the attitudes toward the study of English vary. All ESL situations share, by definition, an imposition of English on the learner and often this is perceived as a derogatory comment on the home culture. The reasons for the various attitudes towards and the learning ESL are ultimately to be found in the social settings.

Bilingual Education

The domain of bilingual education within the area of TESOL, refers to programmes where equal emphasis is placed on learning the native language as well as English. The goals of bilingual education are maintenance of bilingual education programmes, where the programmes offer not only the native language but also the native cultures. There is very little systematic knowledge of techniques and procedures for teaching children a second language at the elementary level, which is coherent to the theory of language acquisition.

English to Speakers of Other Dialects

The last domain of TESOL refers to ESOD (English to Speakers of Other Dialects) or more commonly known as SESD (Standard English as a Second Dialect). Standard English as a second dialect deals with teaching English to those, whose native language is a distinct English dialect which differs markedly from standard English, such as the Maoris in New Zealand, the native Americans in Alaska and Canada. Even though the social settings differ widely, the educational problems remain markedly similar. There were attempts to adopt foreign language teaching techniques, but such methods have not turned out very well. Some major issues have been: (a) applying linguistic descriptions to studies of interference in reading and writing and consequent implications for teaching; (b) teaching the legitimacy of the dialects as a linguistic system in its own right; (c) the identification of culture-specific speech acts and the legitimacy of the culture itself; and (d) language attitudes.

The domains of TESOL range over a wide variety of situations and needs. The specific situation of the learner needs to be taken into account as the social, political, culture and economic factors tend to be of far more significance in influencing educational results than any other language teaching methods.

Foreign language teaching turns primarily to psychology for theory, models, and explanatory frameworks. With the recent focus on student learning rather than on teaching, cognitive pscyhology has succeeded behavioural psychology as a more viable approach. In general, language teaching remains electic in its methods. The audio-lingual method has been discredited. There is a plethora of methods, among which may be mentioned community counselling-learning, notional-functional syllabi, rapid acquisition etc. These methods vary widely, and each has its advantages and disadvantages. Actually, as long as teachers and students have confidence in teaching and learning and all are happy in the process, methods do not make too much difference. By far the most important development in TESOL has been the emphasis on a communicative approach in language teaching (Coste 1976, Widdowson, 1978). It is certain that everyone feels the necessity to use language for communicative purposes. Consequently, the concern for teaching linguistic competence has widened to include communicative competence and teaching methods reflect this shift. One more development in TESOL deserves mention, namely the publication of 'A Grammar of Contemporary English' (1972) and its shorter version, 'A Concise Grammar of Contemporary English' by Quirk and Greenbaum (1973), which provide a wealth of information for the English teachers, textbook writers and students alike.

Process of Language Learning

The criteria for successful language learning depend on the learner, his circumstances and purposes. The process of learning which address the psychological mechanisms responsible for learning, cannot be considered in isolation from these factors. The concept of successful mastery varies enormously, and so a description of 'proficiency' is logically prior to the consideration of process descriptions of language learning. There is the evidence of at least two components of language proficiency for second language learners. The learners, for example, who studied a language in classrooms, yet seemed particularly ill equipped to communicate in the streets, or the immigrants whose control of the new language permitted flawless negotiations in the streets fail to be proficient under more formal conditions of examination system. Such examples are problematic to a concept of proficiency which requires a single assessment of mastery to bind the learner to a particular stage in language acquisition.

One approach to the description of proficiency has been to devise a scheme in which the global concept of proficiency is analysed into isolable component skills, which can be independently involved to describe proficiency in specific situations.

For foreign language education, the most productive division of abilities has distinguished communicative language competence from academic language competence. The former refers to the ability to use language for interpersonal functions in informal settings. The latter refers to the ability to use language for its ideational functions, as a tool of thought, in accordance with the conventions of text and other formalized uses of language. The role of the determinants of achievement becomes more systematic when proficiency is defined in more specialized ways. One application of this distinction of aspects of proficiency is in understanding the role of age in second language learning.

In global judgements of proficiency, the tendency is to compare the second language learner with a native speaking peer. Thus, children may be assessed in terms of their ability to communicate on the playground, while adults would be required to participate in mature conversations and use the language to manage their lives with competence in the literate forms of the language. When attention is paid to these aspects of proficiency required by the two age-groups, comparisons between adults and children show quite different patterns.

The need for a distinction between communicative and academic uses of language is supported by study of the success or failure of language learners, who appear to know the language well when communicating with their peers, yet fail in school tests where more specialized uses of the language are required. These relationships have been reported in a variety of language teaching programmes in different countries of the world. In general, attention must be paid to the criteria by which proficiency will be established for a learner in a given situation. Using a language is complex, and judgements of the ability to carry out that skill must reflect that complexity.

The process of language learning can be described as the interaction between the determinants of achievement and the concept of proficiency. In cognitive terms, the mechanism underlying the acquisition of knowledge are the same, but the specific outcomes of learning in terms of effectivity in learning and developing specific linguistic skills depend upon the factors of achievement. The process itself can never be observed directly but only described inferentially in terms of the type of skill which is developed.

The models of learning process based on psychological principles explain the relationship between determinants of achievement and aspects of proficiency from the perspective of the language learner. These models vary in detail; some being based more directly on cognitive developmental models or information processing models. One of the earliest cognitive models was the "creative construction hypothesis," proposed by Dulay and Burt (1974). They argued that a second language is constructed in much the same way as a child constructs a first language — input is organised in terms of a cognitive apparatus which is designed to respond to meanings. This requirement for construction precludes influences such as language transfer from first language knowledge or comparison between the two languages, first and second. The primary constraint on order and case of acquisition in a second language is cognitive, and the effects of linguistic factors such as similarity between languages and social factors such as, environmental constraints, are minimized. One of the problems with the creative construction hypothesis is that it underestimates the influence of instruction and the possibility of a learner profiting by inter-lingual comparisons. Consequently Krashen (1981) proposed a model in which two processes are identified — acquisition, which corresponds roughly to the creative construction process; and learning, which incorporates intervention, either by the learner or some instructional programme. Krashen argues that these two processes are distinct and the knowledge accrued by each is functionally differentiated. Specifically, the language which is acquired can be used as a response initiator and is the source of most spontaneous uses of language. The language which is learnt, by contrast, can function only as a "monitor" for the purpose of editing speech under restricted conditions. While Krashen's model succeeds in accounting for second language learning, the explanation has a number of theoretical problems. McLaughlin (1978) pointed out the difficulties with the underlying cognitive mechanisms, and Sharwood Smith (1981) pointed out the categorical nature of the language learning acquisition dichotomy. Nevertheless, the model has succeeded in stimulating interesting discussion about the cognitive processes responsible for second or foreign language learning.

Most models of the language learning process allow a role for the learner to intervene in the learning task and take some responsibility for progress in language learning. The outcome is a set of "strategies" for language learning, which may operate at either a conscious or an unconscious level. Learning, productive, communicative and receptive strategies have been identified with the characteristics of successful language learners. These strategies have been examined empirically for their specific effect on language learning (Bialystok, 1979). The findings of all these enquiries is that learners can actively participate in the language learning process and influence the outcomes in a positive way through the adoption of efficient strategies. Finally, most current models of the language learning process attempt to account for proficiency in the ways identified as communicative or formal. Krashen, for example, constructs a profile of the type of learner and the type of environment, that is more likely to promote the development of one or the other aspects of proficiency. Emphasis on learning results in formal language proficiency while emphasis on language acquisition resulting in communicative language proficiency.

The language learning process which isolates aspects of proficiency provides only a rough framework in which more specific questions may be raised. For example, the age of the learner can be reformulated as a relationship between a certain type of learner, who has particular cognitive and linguistic limitations and the type of proficiency that learner is expected to achieve. The questions of stages of learning must be restated in terms of more specific descriptions of proficiency. The role of the environment is obviously crucial to language learning, but the most likely effect of such factors is on the ease and enjoyability of the task rather than the process. It is unlikely that the human mind incorporates a new language in fundamentally different ways from the procedures for learning other information. It is to those models that researchers must look for clues to the questions posed about how people learn foreign languages.

The History of Foreign Language Teaching

Certain well defined trends in methodological approaches to foreign language teaching can be noted throughout history. As a generalisation it can be said that the oldest way of teaching langauge was through the direct method and text interpretation. After the Renaissance, the tendency was to centre teaching upon grammatical theory and translation; functional methods became a focus of interest towards the end of the nineteenth century. Since the early 1960s, there was the tendency for an integrated approach.

Foreign language teaching in ancient times (2500 BC - AD 900) was characterized by exclusive emphasis on the learning of the living language through oral conversation or text analysis. From the Renaissance to the eighteenth century, Latin, Greek and Arabic fulfilled the role of *'lingua franca'* in different parts of the world. They were learnt mainly through direct contact with the written texts or "classics", and grammar was mainly considered in terms of Quintilian's idea of text interpretation. Latin, Greek and Arabic were the languages of theology, philosophy, literature and science.

At the beginning of the nineteenth century there was a resurgence of grammar. Then came the so-called Reform Movement in Europe and the United States and the direct method or natural method was strongly advocated by educators and theoreticians. Starting from the 1920s, new ideas and principles for language teaching were developed within the theoretical orientations of the oral approach, structural linguistics, and the various forms of the communicative approach (Titone, 1968).

At present the main tendency is to combine, either in theory or in practice, the experience and principles of various methods according to a kind of eclecticism as an "integrated approach." A major impact has been made upon methodology by the contributions of the communication sciences and educational psychology. A large body of research findings from applied linguistics and pscyholinguistics have helped teachers towards more effective lines of action.

Foreign Language Teaching Policy

The crucial role of language for individuals, social groups, and states has made it important for states to define national language policies. Depending on their internal linguistic situation, the relative political power of various linguistic groups, views on language rights and language equality, and other factors; the states may choose to promote a policy of a unilingual, bilingual or multilingual society. This general language policy, with explicit statutory legitimation (e.g., Canada and Finland) or implicit social legitimation by tradition (e.g., the United States), is one of the major determinants of a nation's language teaching policy. Another major determinant is the nation's political and economic orientation towards other nations, which partly explains the language teaching policy in some countries, specially after the Second World War. The term, "foreign language teaching policy" refers to the plans and practical measures undertaken to fulfill a country's needs for knowledge of foreign languages. The need to teach citizens to understand and use either a second language or a foreign language arises from language contacts both within the country and with other countries.

Systematic attempts to define a national policy of foreign language teaching are of a relatively recent origin. The fact that the teaching of foreign languages has expanded to encompass larger sections of the population including both younger and adult learners means that language teaching has become increasingly more institutionalised. It has become more organised and systematic with the roles and tasks being specified in greater detail. Language teaching is not just the activity of individual teachers; it is a system of activities at several levels. In order to understand language teaching in all its complexity, it is necessary to be aware of its various levels and subsystems and of their interrelationships. It is also necessary to relate language teaching to its broader educational and societal context.

The organisations all over the world have contributed to exploring problems related to defining national language teaching policies. Two seminars sponsored by the UNESCO Institute for Education in the 1960s, addressed problems related to an early start of foreign langauge teaching. Since the early 1960s, the Council of Europe has actively worked for the improvement of foreign language teaching in Europe. Through a number of seminars, symposia, and projects, its work has stimulated foreign language teaching in member countries. The Helsinki Accords (1975) urges the signatory states "to encourage the study of foreign languages and civilization as an important means of expanding communication among peoples."

Components of Foreign Language Teaching Policy

As linguistic conditions and social systems differ, foreign language teaching policy may range from an explicit, detailed, and binding document to implicit tradition. Thus each country will have to decide what criteria its foreign langauge teaching policy has to fulfill.

The first stage in defining a foreign language teaching policy usually consists of assessing the country's need for people with a requisite type and extent of knowledge of different languages. Several studies conducted in Sweden in the early 1960s, were among the first systematic attempts at needs assessment. Since then a number of needs assessments have been carried out in several countries. They have dealt with language needs in business and industry. Recently more detailed methods have been developed for identifying the needs of people learning foreign languages (Richterich and Chancerel, 1980).

Another major area of planning is related to continuity in language teaching and learning. The Finnish Commission outlined, in broad terms, the general approach of teaching and the general progression of objectives on different levels of the educational system. Such an outline is designed to improve articulation in different types and levels of educational institutions which provide language learning services.

Foreign language teaching policy has also to tackle the quantitative and qualitative targets of language teaching. It may be found useful to estimate how many people will need to know particular languages and what are the languages they will need to learn. After the scope and general orientation of language teaching has been determined, there is a need to set up an efficient administration and organisation to take care of the initial and in-service education of language teachers, to promote syllabus design and materials construction, and to make language learning services available from compulsory education to adult education (Strevens, 1977). The system of language teaching is a complex whole. Its successful performance requires continuous research, development and evaluation as well as a close link between theory and practice. Foreign language teaching policy is designed to coordinate all these activities and to help langauge teaching become a self-corrective system.

Language and Language Teaching

Foreign language teaching since the 1950s, has gone through three main cycles, each of which has been affected by theories of language, linguistics and learning.

Structural linguistics, combined with some behaviourist theories of learning to produce methods of teaching which were variously called, 'the audio-lingual method,' 'the direct method' and 'the S-R (Stimulus-Response) approach.' The main ideas of these approaches are:

(a) Language is speech, not writing;

(b) A language is a set of habits;

(c) Teachers should teach the language, not about the language;

(d) Languages are varied.

The ideas of contrastive linguistics and contrastive analysis were also influential in persuading many language teachers about teaching that "those elements that are similar to his native language will be simple for him, and those elements that are different will be difficult" (Lado, 1957), and that the way to find out differences is through scientific contrastive analysis of the native language of the speaker and the target language to be learnt, particularly as regards phonemic differences between the languages being contrasted (Dension, 1962).

The audio-lingual theory has the following principal ideas: (a) that since speech is primary and writing secondary, the habits to be learnt must be learnt first of all as auditory discrimination responses and speech responses; (b) that habits must be automatized as much as possible so that they can be called forth without conscious attention; (c) that the automatization of habits occurs chiefly by practice, that is, by repetition. (Carroll, 1965). Chomsky, however, reacted sharply both to the linguistic and to the psychological views on which the audio-lingual method was based. He did not accept that language was a set of habits and described the "rule-governed creativity involved in the everyday use of language" (Chomsky, 1964), while pointing out that if language is "generative," it cannot be learnt merely as a set of habits. Although Chomsky's work was difficult for teachers to access, this description of language as "rule-governed behaviour" revived the old arguments about grammar-translation method versus a more direct method approach. Carroll described the 'cognitive-code learning theory', which may be thought of as a modified grammar-translation theory. According to this theory, learning a language is a process of acquiring conscious control of the phonological, grammatical, and lexical patterns of a second language largely through study and analysis of these patterns as a body of knowledge (Carroll, 1965).

A combination of an 'S-R' and a "generative" approach was seen as a resolution of these above two points of view in teaching language (Dunlop, 1970) and "a meaningful synthesis" was suggested in Carroll's "cognitive habit-formation theory" (Carroll, 1971). Lenneberg's biological theory of language had also stated that primary language acquisition occurs between the ages of two and three years and puberty by "an interaction of maturation and self-programmed learning," which implies that human beings have a language learning mechanism, which is referred as "language acquisition device." After puberty, the ability for self-organisation and adjustment to the physiological demands of verbal behaviour quickly declines (Lenneberg, 1967). The implication of Lenneberg's theory for foreign language learning is that until the child reaches the age of puberty, his innate language learning ability will enable it to structure the foreign language being learnt; whereas after that age (for example, in adult learning) this innate language learning ability would decline and the adult learner would need a more structural approach to learning a foreign language and need more explanation of the rules governing the foreign language. Another implication of Lenneberg's theory is that a distinction needs to be made between different approaches to language learning and teaching languages at different levels — a distinction, which is not always made clear.

In the 1970s and early 1980s, the third cycle of modern langauge teaching concerns "communicative competence." Here language competence is seen as including:

(a) Formal possibility (i.e., grammatically possible sentence);

(b) Feasibility (i.e., a sentence may be possible grammatically but hardly feasible);

(c) Appropriateness to context;

(d) Possibility of occurrence (Hymes, 1970).

The notional-functional syllabus (Wilkins, 1976) concentrates on language for the communication needs of the learner and these will include social behaviours as well as grammatical competence at the level of performance, and appropriateness of language to the situations (van EK, 1975).

Communicative competence is still an aim rather than a reality in the classroom and "learner-centred" learning is very often the focal point here with approaches like community language learning. The idea of individual learning strategies attracts attention, no doubt, and so does the individualized work with the learner in language learning situations. In this context, computers in language teaching are attracting attention and CALL (Computer-Assisted Language Learning) includes, among other things, games and simulations; interactive audio and video; conventional language teaching exercises; and the application of business software to language learning activities.

Inductive Versus Deductive Foreign Langauge Teaching

The inductive and deductive approaches in foreign and second langauge teaching refer to procedures for introducing material in teaching. Inductive approach introduces the students to a number of examples from which they develop a rule or generalization which governs the examples. Deductive approach introduces the students to a statement, generalization or rule and allows them to provide specific examples, applications and practice. The specific examples are deducted from the general rule.

The history of second/foreign language teaching methodology has witnessed an ongoing debate concerning the preferability of inductive or deductive approach. The debate is related to other controversies in the field, such as formal versus informal language learning and the function which language rules play in the learning process.

Historically, different teaching methods have been associated with either the inductive or the deductive approach. The formalists who tend to focus on language analysis have relied mostly on deductive approach, while activists, while stressing langauge use, have relied more on inductive approach. The grammar-translation method is generally associated with the deductive approach, since grammar is taught explicitly and is viewed as a significant teaching goal. The direct method is usually associated with the inductive approach since it focuses on structural practice and students are left to form their own generalizations about grammatical structures based on what they have been practicing. In the audio-lingual approach the language learner has been encouraged to induce grammatical rules. The cognitive-code approach calls for a return to explaining grammar rules first. It has been claimed that this approach involves students' reasoning processes in language learning. The approach in the present era is concerned with communication and use of langauge according to the specific needs of the learner. It emphasizes inductive learning since the learner is encouraged to induce information from real-life experiences to form generalizations.

The inductive/deductive approach is not limited to teaching grammar but applies to other areas in language teaching as well. In teaching reading, for example, students can be encouraged to seek comprehension by inferring meaning of unknown words from the context (inductive approach), or by referring to a bilingual dictionary for unknown words (deductive approach). Proponents of the inductive approach believe that it facilitates the induction of underlying abstractions of the language and that the learner understands better when he/she discovers the underlying abstraction for himself or herself, which increases learner's retention. Proponents of the deductive approach believe that introducing the rule at the beginning allows the learner to apply the rule during the practice session of the learning situation rather than to spend time confirming the hypothesis.

The strongest criticism of the two approaches is that they must be viewed in relation to other variables, such as, the conditions of learning, the learning situation, the learning material, the subject matter and the learner himself. The learner's goal in learning the language, his age, learning style, aptitude, and strategies influence his ability to utilize generalizations or rules made available by the deductive approach. For the inductive approach, it is necessary to be able to identify certain attributes of the learning concept. It requires careful consideration to determine whether these approaches are justified to mark a significant difference in language teaching and learning situations.

The Eclectic Method

Eclecticism, a mode of thought which emerges from various philosophical systems, attempts into a logically coherent unity in second language teaching. The eclectic method tends to be adopted by those who wish to avoid rigid commitments. The eclectic approach, whether in its passive form or in its more active form, has much to commend from a practical point of view and tends to emerge at times when established schools of thought have become dogmatic. Eclecticism is a position favoured by practical-minded teachers, who like to experiment with new ideas, but also need to reconcile with the need to maintain a set of techniques to work in a particular learning situation. The eclectic approach in language teaching has a long history. The eclecticists are willing to experiment in a learning situation and seek to maintain a judicious balance in teaching and gradually evolve a method which suits the circumstances.

Much recent work has emphasized the fact that language learners manifest a great variety of background personalities, and individual learning styles. It follows that there can be no single method or theory, which is capable of accounting for all aspects of language and language learning. It is claimed that emphasis should be placed on the responsibility of individual teachers to make informed, intelligent choices from a large number of competing methodologies available to them.

In his 'Principles of Language Study' (1922), Palmer recognised that language teaching is an art rather than a science, and that there are bound to be disagreements about the best procedure to adopt to achieve a particular end. If the varying needs of students are to be taken into account, it is essential that a dogmatic theorizing should be avoided and a varied and flexible approach should be followed to classroom methodology of language teaching. Palmer suggests that a method of teaching should be developed in which both inductive and deductive principles are used in the teaching programme. The application of this principle, which Palmer calls the "multiple line of approach," results in a cycle of activities in which the various learning principles support and complement one another. According to Palmer, only in this way can justice be done to the richness of language and provision be made for the many and diverse needs of the learner. A cyclical, interaction model, as advocated by Palmer tends to be preferred by those who recognise the need to reconcile on a practical level approach, for example, cognitive-code learning theory and audio-lingual habit theory, or structural, functional, and experimental concepts of curriculum. This reconciliation is brought about by adopting a combination of teaching strategies with varying degrees of emphasis depending on the teacher's assessment of the students' needs.

The Notional-Functional Syllabus

The notional-functional syllabus is an approach to language syllabus design and therefore concerns decisions leading to the organisation and selection of langauge content for teaching/learning purposes. The early proponents of the notional-functional syllabus presented it as an analytic approach to syllabus organisation (Wilkins, 1976), which does not view language components as building blocks to be accumulated progressively but as types of language behaviour which represent the global way in which people use language. The term "notions" in the notional-functional syllabus refers to concepts which people use in verbal communication and hence it represents a wide variety of levels of abstraction; general notions related to universal themes such as time, space, motion, and so on, while specific notions are topic-related, for example, travel, sports, work and so on. The term "function" refers to the functional meaning of an utterance, that is, the social purpose of that utterance. The notional-functional syllabus is organised in terms of the purposes for which people are learning language and the kinds of language performance that are necessary to meet those purposes (Wit Kins, 1976). The notional-functional syllabus began as a new trend in the United Kingdom and Europe during the early 1970s and was first realized in syllabus format with the publication of van Ek's (1975) 'Threshold Level' of language proficiency for the Council of Europe, which had a widespread influence in popularising functional syllabi for the language learners.

The influence of psychological factors on language learning comes primarily from two sources: individual variation in a learner's success with the task and the more universal constraints that govern human learning.

Typically, language teaching in schools is organised into a number of lessons per week for a number of years. The methods that attempt to immerse the learners in the foreign language are a form of organisation that has been likened to "gardening in a gale" (Hawkins, 1981): the tender seedlings of the foreign language, planted and nurtured by the classroom teacher for 40 or 50 minutes, are exposed to the native language that blows across them as soon as the classroom doors are open. It has been suggested that if the number of hours of instruction that a language learner gets are concentrated into a shorter period without the distracting interruptions of other subjects and languages, then the learning would be more effective. Such intensive courses are difficult to reconcile with the other demands of the school curriculum and are therefore not common at the school level of language learning, though there have been experiments with them (Hawkins, 1988).

The language learning in schools may be made more intensive not only by increasing the number of hours per week. devoted to teaching the foreign language but also by teaching other subjects through the medium of the foreign language. Experiments along these lines have taken place in a number of countries. The role of the environment is obviously crucial to language learning, but the most likely effect of such factor is on the ease and enjoyability of the task rather than the process.

HPH

BIBLIOGRAPHY

(1) Allen, Virginia French and Forman Sidney, (1967), *English as a Second Language,* Teachers College Press, New York.

(2) Allwright R, (1979), *Language Learning through Communication Practice,* Oxford University Press, London.

(3) Bachman L.F and Palmer A.S., (1966), *Language Testing in Practice,* Oxford University Press, Oxford.

(4) Brown, H Douglas, (1994), *Teaching by Principles: An Interactive Approach to Language Pedagogy.* Prentice Hall Regents, Englewood Cliffs, New Jersey.

(5) Brumfit, (1988), *Communicative Language Teaching,* Cambridge University Press, Cambridge.

(6) Byme Donn, (1980), *English Teaching Perspectives,* Longman, U.K.

(7) Gagne R.M., (1965), The Conditions of Learning, Holt, Rinehart and Winston, New York.

(8) Hinsdale B.A. (1898), *Teaching the Language Arts: Speech, Reading, Composition,* D. Appleton and Company, New York.

(9) Hornberger Nancy H, Springer, (2009), *General Editor, Encyclopedia of Language and Education,* 2nd Edition, Vol. 4, Academic Press, Oxford, U.K.

(10) *International Encyclopedia of Education,* Vol. 1, third edition, (2010), Elsevier, Academic Press, Oxford, U.K.

(11) Krashen S.D., (1981), *Second Language Acquisition and Second Language Learning,* Oxford University Press, Oxford.

(12) Krashen S.D. & Terrell T. (1983), *The Natural Approach: Language Acquisition in the Classroom,* Pergamon Press, Oxford.

(13) Morn Bob, Ben Perietz Miriam and Brown Sally, Editors, (2000), *International Companion to Education,* Routledge, London & New York.

(14) Nunan D. (1989), *Designing Tasks for the Communicative Classroom,* Cambridge University Press, Cambridge.

(15) Prabhu (1987), *Second Language Pedagogy,* Oxford University Press, Oxford.

(16) Richards J.C. (2001), *Curriculum Development in Language Teaching,* Cambridge University Press, Cambridge.

(17) Spolsky B. (1989), *Conditions for Second Language Learning,* Oxford University Press, Oxford.

(18) Spolsky B. (1995), *Measured Words,* Oxford University Press, Oxford.

(19) Vygotsky L.S. (1962), *Thought and Language,* MIT Press, Cambridge, Massachusetts.

HPH

INDEX

HPH